MAN EATERS

Also by Rupert Matthews in
Piccolo True Stories

Crazy Crimes

MANEATERS

RUPERT MATTHEWS

A PICCOLO ORIGINAL
Piccolo Books

First published 1990 by Pan Books Ltd,
Cavaye Place, London SW10 9PG

9 8 7 6 5 4 3 2

© Rupert Matthews 1990
Illustrations © Pan Books Ltd 1990

ISBN 0 330 31060 7

Phototypeset by Input Typesetting Ltd, London

Printed and bound in Great Britain by
Richard Clay Ltd, Bungay, Suffolk

CONTENTS

MANEATERS – AN INTRODUCTION

To be faced by a maneater is a terrifying experience, bringing with it the threat of terrible pain and sudden death. In the eyes of a maneater victims see only hunger and anger, never the docile obedience humans are used to from pets. It is the sheer power of the maneater and its hostility to humans which makes it such a frightening and disturbing phenomenon.

Before the days of television and radio, people would gather round their fires at night and tell terrifying stories about the dangerous beasts of the forest. They told how ferocious wolves or tigers loved nothing better than to pounce on unwary humans and gobble them up. Such tales helped to pass the long dark evenings, but few people bothered to check how much truth they contained. The people simply did their best to kill the dangerous animals.

More recently the whole subject of maneating has become more controversial as scientists and conservationists have become concerned for the wildlife of the world. They report how various types of animal are nearly extinct, and how we can save them. In many cases animals which have long been known to attack humans have become very rare and so some conservationists prefer to ignore stories of maneating and to emphasize the ecological role of the animal concerned. But the maneaters refuse to be ignored or to go away.

Some of the most exciting real-life encounters between humans and maneating animals are retold in this book. There are the lone tigers which hunted humans with a frightening dedication over several months, devouring hundreds of humans; packs of wolves driven by hunger to prey on the humans they usually avoid and sharks who look on swimmers as just another type of food.

All the events in this book are true, based upon eyewitness accounts by the people involved. We meet humans preyed on by ferocious beasts, villages living in terror of the night, and we meet the brave men who set out to kill the maneaters, sometimes only to become prey themselves.

In reading these exciting tales it is important to realize that such beasts are very uncommon; most animals, even powerful hunters, prefer to avoid humans. Throughout the whole world months may pass without a single maneating animal attacking a human, but when a maneater does strike, it can kill dozens, or even hundreds of people before it is caught or killed.

KILLERS IN THE NIGHT

Leopards

The leopard hunts at night, resting in trees or beside forest tracks, waiting for a victim to come its way. When it pounces, the leopard is a ferocious beast, far more powerful for its size than other great cats. Its feet are equipped with long, razor-sharp claws which can strike down a victim in seconds. The powerful jaws of the leopard carry long, pointed teeth which can inflict fatal wounds with startling speed. Often the prey of a leopard is dead before it can utter a sound.

The coat of the leopard makes it one of the most distinctive animals in the world. The pale yellow fur is dotted with black spots, arranged in small rings known as rosettes. Some leopards have small rosettes close together, while others have large rosettes spaced far apart. Some leopards are completely black and are known as black panthers. These creatures are rare and almost completely invisible in the jungle night. When seen in bright sunlight, however, the black panther can be seen to have rosettes just like those of normal leopards. They are seen as dull splotches on an otherwise glossy coat.

Unlike most other large carnivores, the leopard still lives in most of its original homelands and is common in Africa south of the Sahara as well as in much of Asia, including India, Siberia and China. Until a few hundred years ago the leopard was found in Europe, even in Britain, but is now extinct in these areas. Despite its widespread range, the leopard is now much rarer than it once was. It is difficult to know exactly how many leopards live in a particular region, but locals in most areas see leopards much less than they did about fifty years ago.

Usually the leopard avoids contact with man, though it has a poor sense of smell and can be tracked without much difficulty. However, this great cat has the unfortunate habit of hanging around forest villages and enjoys eating food scraps left over from human meals, often visiting rubbish dumps. The leopard is also fond of eating dogs, which it will hunt in villages at night.

The leopard is, therefore, used to being close to humans. Sometimes a leopard will cease avoiding humans, and will actively begin to hunt them. This usually happens when a leopard is disturbed, perhaps when stalking a dog, or if it is angry, the leopard will lash out and even kill. Under such circumstances the leopard can gain a liking for human flesh and will avoid its normal prey to hunt humans. It becomes a maneater.

This is almost certainly what happened to a leopard in Almora, northern India, in 1906. The leopard was a big male, powerfully built and quite able to kill any animal it might meet in the forest. Until it was fully grown, the leopard hunted forest animals, but one night it entered Almora village looking for food on the rubbish tip.

As the leopard moved through the darkness it came across a man. The man saw the leopard at the same moment, but mistook it for a dog trying to creep into his house.

'Yah,' he shouted, throwing a piece of firewood at the creature. 'Get away dog.'

The wood struck the leopard on the snout causing it to snarl angrily. The man realized what the animal was and turned to flee. But the leopard was too quick for him, springing and clawing him to the ground. The jaws closed over the man's neck, killing him instantly. The village was silent. Nobody had heard the man die. The leopard sniffed the unfamiliar smell of human flesh, then it began to eat. The leopard of Almora had become a maneater.

After this incident the leopard began hunting humans deliberately. Eventually it abandoned its normal prey of deer and small animals, and ate only humans. During the following four years it killed and ate more than 400 people. An average of one every three nights.

The Almora maneater spread fear through the forests, causing villagers to stay indoors at night and only to travel if they needed to do so. The bloody career of the leopard came to an end in April 1910 after a particularly savage attack a few miles west of Almora.

The victims were a young farmer named Salan and his wife who lived in a solitary hut some miles from the nearest village. Salan had been given a small patch of land in a remote valley when he had married two months earlier and had built his house on the land. The recent weeks had been very hot and humid and Salan had taken to the habit of leaving the front door and rear window of his hut open to create a pleasant through draught of cooler air, but it also left him open to the creatures of the jungle and especially vulnerable to an attack from the leopard.

As usual, Salan stacked his farming tools against the far wall of the hut and lay down to sleep beside his wife. The sun set beyond the nearby hills, plunging the hut into darkness. As the couple slept the moon rose above the hills, casting a soft light across the forest.

Salan was roused from deep sleep by a choking sound. Something fell across his chest and grabbed him. He opened his eyes, looked round and gasped in horror. A huge leopard was in the doorway, dragging his wife outside while she was holding on to Salan's chest.

Salan was terrified, but knew he must act quickly to save his wife. He leapt to his feet and grabbed hold of his wife's waist, bracing his leg against the doorpost. The leopard tugged, but Salan held on tightly to his wife. The leopard snarled with all the savagery of an angry hunter. It pulled again and the woman gasped in panic. Salan felt his grip slipping and was petrified that he would lose his wife to the leopard. Bringing his other leg round against the wall Salan tightened his grip.

At that moment, the leopard changed its grip on its prey. Salan tugged hard, dragging his wife into the room, while the leopard, caught off balance, tumbled backwards. Salan saw his chance and leapt forwards. He slammed the door and threw the bolts shut. He collapsed on the floor, but then remembered that the window was open. Springing up, Salan ran across the room and crashed the shutters into place, just as the leopard ran to the opening.

Turning to his wife, Salan found she was badly cut around the throat, but she was still alive. He cut up a shirt to make a bandage, wrapping it around the wounds and the bleeding soon stopped. His wife smiled weakly, but could not speak.

All night long the leopard continued to prowl around the house. Salan occasionally heard it push against the door, or scratch at the wooden walls. As dawn broke in the eastern sky the leopard left, to hide in the nearby forest.

Cautiously Salan opened the door. Pale sunlight bathed the field in front of his house. The leopard was nowhere to be seen. Gripping his harvesting knife, the only weapon he had, Salan stepped on to the verandah. Still there was no sign of the man-eater. He collected a mug of water from the barrel on the verandah and took it to his wife, who drank eagerly.

Salan was worried. He knew that his wife badly needed medical help, but he did not want to leave her alone. He was certain that if he left, the leopard would return to kill her. All day long he sat on the verandah, waiting for someone to come along the lonely track which passed his house.

Finally, as the sun sank during the late afternoon, Salan heard voices. Out of the jungle walked a British officer carrying a powerful rifle, followed by several servants carrying pieces of luggage. Help at last!

Salan ran forwards and welcomed the stranger, pouring out his story of the night of terror. Colonel Jim Corbett listened to Salan with interest. He had been sent by the government to kill the man-eating leopard but had spent several months in the jungle without any success. This was the first time he had been so close to the killer. When he learnt that the injured woman was still alive, Corbett raced into the house. He opened his medical chest and cleaned the wounds as best he could. Then he asked Salan to tell him exactly what had happened the night before.

When Salan had finished, Corbett sat back to think. He guessed that the leopard was still nearby, for leopards do not move far during the day, and it had been at the hut until dawn. Corbett had pursued many maneaters in recent years and knew them to be extremely dangerous and difficult creatures to hunt, but he also knew that they rarely passed up the chance of an easy kill. Corbett decided to set a trap.

He sent some of his men to a nearby village to buy a goat, then began walking around the forest near the hut. Not far away was a patch of very dense jungle where no birds or deer could be found. Corbett guessed that the leopard was resting there, though he could not see it.

Satisfied with his patrol, Corbett returned to Salan's hut to find his servants had returned with the goat. He told them to tie the goat to a stake near the edge of the field, while he climbed into a nearby tree. He told his servants to tie strong thorn branches to the rear of the platform in case the leopard climbed the tree.

Then he sat down with his gun on his knees and waited.

Soon after midnight the goat began bleating in fear and staring at something in the forest. Corbett could not see what the goat was watching, but guessed it must be the leopard. The goat slowly backed around as the leopard moved, making it clear that the leopard was heading for Corbett.

Corbett could see nothing, but suddenly the thorn branches around the tree rustled. The leopard was in the tree and was pulling at the barrier. With a tremendous tug the leopard wrenched the thorns to one side, but they sprang back into place. Beads of cold sweat broke out on Corbett's face. He knew that if the leopard got through the barrier, it would kill him. The leopard growled in anger and pulled at the branches again. They held firm.

Jumping down from the tree, the leopard made for the goat. In the dense darkness, Corbett could not see the leopard at all, but he could see the faint white smudge of the goat. As Corbett strained his eyes in the darkness, he saw the goat leap sideways. There was a savage snarl, a frightened bleat, and then silence. The leopard had killed the goat.

Corbett raised his gun, but could not see what to aim at. A dark shadow moved in front of the white body of the goat and Corbett fired at it. An angry snarl showed that he had hit the leopard. Then silence fell again.

For several minutes the silence continued.

Then Corbett heard his servants calling to see if he was all right. Corbett shouted back that he had hit the leopard, but was not certain if he had killed it. He asked the men to come down to the field carrying bright torches.

Minutes later the flaming pine torches carried by the men were illuminating the field. Corbett climbed down and walked over to the dead goat. He could see bloodstains leading away towards the jungle and knew that the leopard was badly hurt.

'The leopard will not come back tonight,' he told the men. 'We can sleep in the house and stalk the leopard in the morning.'

Just as Corbett turned to move towards the house, one of the men screamed and dropped his torch. Corbett swung round, the angry leopard was charging straight at him from the darkness. The bloodstained jaws and claws of the beast were flashing in the air as it bounded forwards, barely ten metres away. Corbett whipped out his gun and fired, the bullet crashing into the leopard's chest, bowling it over. A second shot finished off the beast. The reign of terror of the Almora maneater was over.

Jaguars

Jaguars, like leopards, hunt at night. The jaguar is the largest carnivore of South America. It lives in dense forests and along the banks of rivers. It can be found from southern Argentina as far north as Arizona and New Mexico in the United States. It is generally very secretive, and is rarely seen by humans. However, jaguars often follow humans in the jungle, and sometimes attack. People who live in South American jungles often report attacks by jaguars. The big cat is clearly a dangerous animal.

In the 1890s the Englishman Hyatt Verrill lived in Costa Rica. He carried on his business for most of the year, but when he could take a holiday he travelled through the interior jungles. The dense forests were beautiful and filled with wonderful wildlife, but Verrill knew the jungle could be dangerous so he always carried a powerful rifle on his shoulder.

On one trip Verrill and a friend named Juan Gomes came to a remote jungle village just as dusk was falling. They stopped at an inn for the night and ordered a hot supper. As the two travellers sat eating their evening meal, the landlord came over.

'Excuse me,' said the landlord. 'But I could not help noticing your fine rifles.'

'Thank you,' said Verrill. 'They are good guns, and very accurate.'

'Perhaps you are sportsmen?' asked the landlord.

'Not really,' replied Verrill. 'I carry the gun for protection, not for hunting.'

The landlord's face fell. He glanced at a group of men sitting by the door and shook his head.

'That is a great shame, sir,' he said. 'My friends were hoping you could help them.'

Gomes glanced at the men, who looked like farmers. 'Why?' he asked. 'What's the matter?'

'There is a terrible jaguar living near here,' said the landlord.

'That's right,' said one of the farmers, walking over to join the conversation. 'It is a large beast, which has been eating our cattle for many months, and now it is killing people.'

'Yes,' said the landlord, 'it killed Alfonso's son just two nights ago. We were hoping you could stay to kill the jaguar.'

'I'd like to help,' said Verrill, 'but we are on our way to Limon and we musn't be late.'

'Anyway,' said Gomes, 'we're not very good hunters and the jaguar is a very difficult animal to track down.' The farmers looked disappointed. 'I'll tell you what,' Gomes continued. 'I've got a friend in Limon who is a very good hunter. I shall tell him about your jaguar and ask him to come to shoot it.'

The landlord brightened up. 'Thank you very much, sir,' he said. 'If you will do that for us, you need not pay for your meal. It is free.'

Next morning, just before dawn, Verrill and Gomes mounted their horses. It was a long way to Limon and they wanted to reach it that day, so they had to make an early start. They trotted out of the inn's courtyard just as the sun rose over the hills.

For some time the two men rode past open fields, but then the road plunged into dense jungle. Suddenly, Verrill's horse stopped dead, shaking with fright, and seconds later a huge jaguar bounded into sight. The horses whinnied in terror and became uncontrollable. Verrill's horse reared and bucked, tossing him to the ground. Gomes's mount turned and bolted, flinging him into a patch of bushes.

Bruised and battered, Verrill looked up in time to see the jaguar bounding towards him. He rolled over, brought his rifle to his shoulder and fired. The rifle roared, but the jaguar came running on. Knowing he had only seconds left, Verrill whipped out his sharp machete knife and prepared to face the powerful beast. At that moment the jaguar sprang, its claws reaching out for Verrill's throat.

A gunshot boomed through the forest and the jaguar spun in mid-air, crashing to the ground.

Verrill picked himself up reeling with shock and surprise. 'He's a monster! He nearly killed me! I think I ought to thank you for saving my life.'

Gomes shrugged. 'Think nothing of it,' he said. 'Come on, let's go tell those farmers their jaguar is dead.'

KILLERS OF THE SWAMPS

The largest reptiles in the world are crocodiles and alligators, which can grow up to seven metres in length. These huge, scaly monsters lurk in rivers and swamps where they search for their prey. They are not particularly fussy about what they eat – any animal which comes down to drink or to swim is likely to be attacked.

These large reptiles are well equipped to attack other animals. They have long snouts, with long, needle-sharp teeth which can easily bite through human bodies. Despite their short, squat legs they can move on land with surprising speed when necessary, while their long, muscular tails can propel them through the water faster than a man can swim.

Unlike many other animals, such as tigers and leopards, which normally avoid man, crocodilians do not appear to have learnt that humans can be dangerous. They will usually attack on sight any human foolish enough to venture into crocodile-infested waters. Until this century some villages in Africa lost more people to crocodiles than through any other cause of death.

The recent widespread use of rifles has led to a serious decline in the numbers of crocodiles and alligators. In some areas they have become extinct, and in other areas their numbers have fallen drastically. Many people, including conservationists, believe that

> the rapid decline of crocodilian populations is a tragedy. However, most people who live in crocodile country, and who have lived for years with the threat of attack, are thankful that the animals have gone. The threat of attack remains very real, however, especially in those more remote areas where crocodilians are still found in large numbers.

Hongo threw his wide fishing net. It spun out to form a broad circle before splashing into the sun-drenched waters of Lake Victoria in Africa. Waiting a few seconds to allow the weights to close the mouth of the net, Hongo hauled the net in. As he heaved the wet twine into his boat, Hongo smiled, for the cast had caught nearly a dozen fish. If he continued to catch fish at this rate he would have enough before noon.

After extracting the fish and tossing them to the floor of his canoe, Hongo stepped to the prow of his craft and prepared to throw the net again. He smiled at his friend Banto fishing in his own craft a few metres away.

'Good catching today,' called Hongo.

'Yes,' agreed Banto. 'I've caught nearly enough for today, even allowing for my son's appetite.'

Hongo laughed. Young Igo was famous for his large appetite. He ate twice as much as other children, yet did not become fat; he seemed to burn the food up by dashing around.

Hongo threw his net again. Water droplets flying from the threads caught the sun, sparkling like tiny jewels. As he waited for the net to close, Hongo saw

Banto hurl his great circular net far from his boat. Hauling in the net, Hongo thought that it felt as if he had a large catch. The net seemed heavier than before. Then suddenly the weight had gone.

'That's funny,' he said.

'What is?' called Banto.

'My net felt heavy,' replied Hongo, 'then suddenly it was light again.'

Banto shrugged. 'Perhaps it got caught on a rock or something,' he suggested.

'Maybe,' said Hongo, but he was unconvinced. There were few rocks in that part of the lake. He looked into the murky water trying to find a rock which might have snagged his net.

'Hey,' shouted Banto. 'It feels like I have got a good catch now.'

Hongo looked up and smiled. 'Good,' he shouted.

Suddenly Banto lurched forwards, nearly falling out of his boat.

'I think . . .' he said then started screaming loudly as he pitched headlong into the water. Hongo watched in surprise, thinking that his friend had slipped from his canoe. Banto rose spluttering to the surface of the lake and looked about him.

'Are you all right?' asked Hongo.

Banto swam to the side of his vessel.

'I think so,' he called. 'Something pulled on my net.'

Suddenly the water around Banto erupted in a violent splash and shower of water engulfing Banto in a fountain of spray and foam. As Hongo watched the waters died down to calm. Banto was nowhere in sight, it was as if he had vanished. Then the waters slowly turned red with blood. Hongo stared in horror at the spot where his friend had been, wondering what could have happened.

Slowly, as if rising from the depths, a great, green head came to the surface. The bright yellow eyes of the creature glinted in the sun, then closed and sank beneath the waters. Hongo recognized the beast as a crocodile and he knew that there was no hope for Banto. The crocodile had dragged him beneath the lake.

Sadly Hongo pulled his net in. The far end of the net, where the fish should have been, was torn and rent. Half of one fish, savagely bitten in two, was entangled in the net. Perhaps the crocodile had been attracted by the shoal of fish. It had eaten the fish in Hongo's net and then moved on to Banto's.

Hongo shuddered suddenly. He had felt the crocodile gripping on to his net only seconds before. If the reptile had tugged at his net instead of at Banto's, he would be dead now himself. Hurriedly Hongo paddled his canoe back to shore and ran along the path to his village. He wondered how on earth he would break the news to Banto's wife.

o   o   o

Banto was killed by an African crocodile and this animal has been responsible for hundreds of attacks on human beings, but Africa is not the only place where these animals attack humans. The swamps and estuaries of southeast Asia and Australia's Northern Territory are the home of the ferocious saltwater crocodile. This reptile can grow to over seven metres in length and is more powerful than its African cousin. It is also more likely to attack large animals, including humans.

In 1962 Noel Monkman was cruising up and down the rivers of the Northern Territory of Australia in a large motor boat. He was searching for specimens of the many different types of insect which inhabit the dense forests of the area around Darwin, known as the Top End.

One afternoon, as Monkman chugged slowly upstream on one of the many virtually unexplored rivers of the region, his craft suddenly shuddered from end to end. Leaping to his feet, Monkman pushed past Robert Jackson, who was helping to record the insect finds, and dashed to the bows.

'What is it?' asked Jackson.

'I'm not sure,' replied Monkman, peering over the side of the boat. 'I think we've hit something.'

'Stop the engine,' Jackson called to Smith, who had been hired to steer.

'Righto,' replied Smith, pushing the engine into neutral.

Monkman continued to peer over the side of the boat. The murky water cleared slightly, allowing Monkman to see beneath the surface.

'I see now,' said Monkman. 'We must have struck a log or something. The planks are dented and chipped.'

Jackson came up to stand beside him.

'Is the damage serious?' he asked.

'I can't really tell from here,' said Monkman, 'the water is too muddy. I'll slip over the side and feel around to see if the boat is holed.'

Taking his shoes off, Monkman swung his legs over the side of the boat and lowered himself into the water. Holding on to the side of the boat with one hand, Monkman felt around the hull with the other. He could feel where something had struck the boat, causing the timbers of the hull to splinter and bend. The damage went down further than he could reach.

Shifting his grip on the boat, to hold onto the planking just above water level, Monkman fumbled deeper beneath the surface. He was groping down to the bottom edge of the damage when he was suddenly hauled backwards with enormous force. Taking a great gulp of air, Monkman was dragged beneath the surface; the waters closed over him, enclosing him in a world of dark and murky liquid.

Monkman struggled against the force holding him down, but whatever had hold of him had a firm grip on the back of his shirt. Reaching behind him, Monkman could feel nothing but water. Bewildered and frightened by the turn of events, Monkman realized that it was his shirt which was holding him down. Rapidly running out of breath, Monkman hurriedly tore at his buttons.

His lungs felt as if they would burst with lack of air as he released the final button. As the shirt came undone, Monkman swam up to the surface. He broke into air, gasping for breath, to see Jackson leaning over the side of the boat and, as soon as he saw Monkman appear Jackson threw him a rope. Monkman grabbed hold and was hauled aboard.

Lying gasping on the deck, Monkman gradually regained his breath.

'What happened?' he asked looking up at Jackson, who appeared to be badly frightened.

'It was a croc,' said Jackson. 'I saw it just as it grabbed you from behind. I thought you were a goner.'

'A croc?' exclaimed Monkman.

'Yeah,' said Jackson, 'and a big one too. Are you OK?'

'I think so,' said Monkman sitting up on the deck. 'It grabbed me by the shirt. I got free once I had got out of it.'

o o o

Monkman's narrow escape occurred close to the site one of the most famous encounters with a crocodile on record. In 1983 a man called Fred was travelling in a small boat up the Parramatta River on a trip deep into the outback of the Northern Territory.

As he steered his small motor boat around a bend in the Parramatta, Fred saw a pair of large crocodiles resting on a muddy bank. They appeared to be asleep. One was lying with its mouth open. Throttling back, Fred slowed his boat down as he moved past the creatures.

Seconds later one of them lifted its heavy body from the ground and dashed into the water. The

second creature, wakened by the first, followed it into the river with a mighty splash.

Shifting the engine into top gear, Fred tried to move out of the way of the crocodiles, but they seemed determined to catch him. With powerful strokes they moved quickly to intercept the boat.

Realizing that his small motor could not outstrip the reptiles, Fred reached for his rifle. Slipping a bullet into the chamber, Fred swung round to aim at the leading crocodile, but he was too late. Lunging forwards, the crocodile smashed its teeth into the fragile wooden hull.

With a sickening crunching sound the side of the boat disintegrated before Fred's eyes. The muddy river water surged in, swirling around the stores and provisions. Springing backwards, Fred pushed himself away from the surging waters and on to the side of the boat away from the attacker.

The crocodile swung its powerful jaws sideways and bit again, crushing another section of the boat. Fred knew that the craft was finished, there was no way it could survive the damage done to it. Seeing no other way out, Fred took a deep breath and threw himself over the side.

Keeping a strong grip on his rifle, Fred swam to the shore as fast as he could. Glancing over his shoulder he could see the two crocodiles still attacking the boat as it slid deeper into the water. Scrambling ashore, Fred staggered a short distance from the river bank before sitting down to rest.

He had hurt his arm while swimming ashore; perhaps he had knocked into a submerged log or rock.

Looking back at the river, Fred could see no sign of either his boat or the crocodiles – they had simply vanished in the dark, swirling waters. Everything in the boat had been lost, his food, map, compass and spare boots.

Fred knew that he was in trouble. He was about 1400 kilometres from the nearest town. The distance between was filled with deserts, jungles and swamps. It would take him many days to walk that distance, even if he had possessed a map to show him the direction. All he had to protect him was a rifle, with twelve bullets, and a knife.

Still, thought Fred, there was no point in sitting thinking about it. He stood up and began walking, though he only had a hazy idea of which direction to go. He knew that he had to head northwards, so he began walking towards the sun. Several days later Fred met up with a tribe of Aborigines. They showed him how to find food in the wild land and pointed him in the right direction. Three weeks later he staggered out of the wilderness into a remote outback settlement. He was thin, exhausted and sunburnt, but he was alive, having survived not only man-eating crocodiles, but also the merciless Australian outback.

o o o

Most attacks by crocodiles and alligators on humans are solitary affairs, like the attacks on Monkman and Fred. A single reptile, or perhaps a pair, will attack a person unwary enough to approach the shore or wade through waters infested by the giant reptiles. In 1945 towards the end of World War Two special circumstances occurred which gave rise to a mass attack which has never been equalled, and probably never will.

In February that year British, Australian and Indian troops were slowly pushing the Japanese army out of Burma and surrounding countries. By 17 February the advance had reached the Ramree Peninsula. Over a thousand Japanese troops held the position and before attacking, the British commander laid his plans carefully.

While he was advancing from the neck of the peninsula with tanks and infantry, the commander asked the Royal Navy to bombard the Japanese positions from the sea. When everything was ready the attack began. The combination of naval firepower and infantry attacks proved too much for the Japanese; they retreated back to the swamps around Kyaukpyu at the tip of the peninsula. The Japanese hoped that ships from their fleet would be able to take them off, but the Royal Navy intercepted the rescue vessels.

Two days later the entire Japanese force was trapped in the swamps. As dusk approached, Sergeant Whitson was called to see his commanding officer, Captain Ramsey.

'Yes sir,' said Whitson as he entered the tent.

'I understand you worked as a boatman before the war,' said Captain Ramsey.

'That's right, sir,' said Whitson, wondering what the statement might lead on to.

'I've got a job for a man who can handle a motor boat,' continued Captain Ramsey. 'I want you to take one of the small canvas boats out to the seaward side of the swamps. I'll give you a machine gun and two men. Your job is to stop the Japs escaping in any canoes they might find. Do you think you can handle that?'

'Yes, sir,' said Whitson. He had not used a boat since he had joined up three years earlier. It would be good to feel a boat beneath his feet again.

As dusk drew on Whitson climbed into the small craft with his men and a powerful machine gun. One of the soldiers looked at the frail craft dubiously.

'Do you reckon this thing will float all right, Sarge?' he asked.

'Of course it will,' replied Whitson. 'So long as one of you clumsy oafs don't put your boots through it. Now get in.'

'Righto, Sarge,' said the soldier. 'Come on Dusty, in we get.'

The three men climbed into the boat. Whitson started the motor and they set off away from the coast.

'I'll keep out of rifle range of the swamp,' said Whitson. 'There's no point in letting the Japs take pot shots at us. Now keep your eyes and ears peeled for any sign of Japs launching canoes or boats. If you think you've spotted one shoot straight away.'

'No problem, Sarge,' said Oakshott, settling down behind the machine gun at the prow of the boat.

For some minutes the boat cruised along the fringes of the swamp, without incident. Then a dull thud sounded from far inland. Seconds later a loud explosion erupted from the swamp, sending a sheet of flame high into the sky.

'Looks like the gunners are doing their bit,' commented Whitson.

Another artillery shell slammed into the swamp. Soon a massive barrage was pounding the Japanese positions.

'I think I'll take the boat in closer now,' said Whitson. 'It's getting darker so we should be safe enough.'

As he turned the craft inland, Whitson felt a gentle tug on the steering. The tide had turned and was flowing out of the swamp towards the open ocean. Gently Whitson pushed the boat to within a hundred metres of the shore. He wanted to be certain that he would not miss any craft putting out to sea in the darkness.

The barrage stopped as suddenly as it had begun. Silence crept over the battle area. Darkness settled over the sea and land alike. Whitson and his two men sat quietly in their boat, listening for the sounds of a boat.

'What's that?' whispered Oakshott.

'Where?' asked Whitson.

'Out there,' said Oakshott pointing towards the shore. 'About twenty feet away.'

Whitson strained to see in the darkness. There was something floating in the water.

'It must be a Jap, killed by the barrage and swept out here by the tide,' he said.

Suddenly the water around the body burst up in a welter of spray as if exploding from beneath. The body leapt upwards, twisted and fell back. A pair of long jaws broke through the water, slashing at the water and chomping on the body.

'What's that?' cried Dusty in alarm. The thrashing in the water ceased. A long, sinister shape glided past the boat, circling it and returning towards the swamp.

'It's a crocodile,' said Oakshott. 'I saw one of them at a zoo back in Calcutta when I was on leave two months back.'

Whitson swallowed hard. 'It made short work of the Jap,' he said going pale.

Suddenly a scream echoed across the dark waters. The scream came again, a heart-chilling yell of terror. Then silence. Whitson glanced at his crew in the darkness. Loud splashing noises came from the swamp, followed by another scream.

'What on earth is going on?' asked Whitson as a yelp of horror came from far to their right. There was a sudden burst of gunfire, then more splashing and screaming.

'It's the crocs,' said Oakshott quietly, as if fearful his voice would attract the reptiles. 'They're going for the Japs. There must be a lot of wounded men after the barrage. There'll be plenty of blood in the water, and nothing drives a crocodile crazy like the smell of blood. They'll go for anything that moves.

In that swamp there's no dry land or trees for the Japs to climb onto. They're sitting targets.'

Whitson stared at the dark shore in horror. The idea of men fighting with giant reptiles filled him with revulsion. The terrors of the men trapped in the muddy swamp with the hungry beasts was too awful even to think of.

For several hours the screaming, splashing and gunfire continued to come from the swamps. British troops both in small boats and along the shore side of the swamp heard the dreadful noises, but few guessed at the true horror of the situation.

Towards dawn the terrible noises eventually died down. Silence hung over the swamps of Ramree. As morning wore on a few Japanese troops crept clear of the area. Only twenty men survived out of more than a thousand who had entered the swamp the day before. Never before or since have so many humans fallen prey to crocodiles in one single night.

CHILDSNATCHERS

Most of the animals in this book are large and power-ful beasts which are able to overpower a full grown man and devour him. But there are many other meat-eating animals in the world which are not large enough to do this. They tend to hunt smaller animals, such as rabbits, gophers and young deer. These ani-mals will never attack an adult human, but they can become maneaters nonetheless.

Children and babies are much smaller and weaker than adult humans, and so are unable to fight off hungry hunters as well. Many animals take advan-tage of this to attack children and to carry them off. Many times young children have vanished when they have been left alone for a few minutes. Often they have fallen victim to predators such as hyenas, wolves or wildcats.

Such events usually take place in remote areas, where the natural predators are present in large num-bers. To the killers, the children are just another source of food. The predators which take them are not confirmed maneaters like those tigers which attack humans. This makes them all the more dangerous for nobody can be certain when a child will fall victim to one of the childsnatchers.

The noon sun blazed down fiercely as it had for most of the summer of 1876 as Anne-Marie

Fouvant thrust her trowel into the soil once more and lifted the earth aside before inserting the young cabbage. She had been working in the vegetable patch for some hours now, ever since her husband, Pierre, had left to visit the cows on the high pasture on Mont Claire.

Anne-Marie leaned back and wiped the sweat from her forehead. She glanced up towards the distant slopes of Mont Claire. Several hundred metres above her she could make out the cattle her husband was tending. The Alps were at their best in the summer, offering fine grazing for the cattle and presenting magnificent views of green forests and snow-capped peaks.

A quiet gurgling caught Anne-Marie's attention. She glanced across the vegetable patch to where her young son was sleeping on a blanket in the shade of a fence panel. The baby gurgled again, kicked its legs then sank back into sleep. Anne-Marie was glad that the boy was sleeping; it allowed her to get on with her work.

The box of cabbages was empty, so the young woman strolled back to the shed to collect the next tray of seedlings which needed planting. As she was emerging from the shed, seed tray in hand, Anne-Marie heard a piercing cry. It was the baby.

Wondering what was wrong, Anne-Marie hurried to the vegetable patch. Perhaps the baby needed changing again. When she reached the garden, however, Anne-Marie dropped the tray. 'Oh my God,' she screamed in terror.

Resting on the ground by the baby's blanket was

a huge brown bird. At the sound of Anne-Marie's scream, the bird looked up, its sharp hooked beak open and its beady black eyes staring at the woman unblinkingly. The baby screamed again, and Anne-Marie rushed forwards. Picking up a spade as she ran, Anne-Marie rushed at the bird, hoping to drive it away.

With a slow, unhurried motion the bird spread its huge wings and pushed them back down. The stroke lifted the bird above the ground and a second beat of the powerful wings carried it higher into the air. In a moment of terrible shock, Anne-Marie saw that the eagle was carrying off the baby. The baby screamed again, in pain and terror. Anne-Marie ran up as fast as she could, desperately hoping to reach the eagle in time. But by the time she reached the spot the great bird was high in the sky. Sobbing with grief, she flung the spade at the departing bird hoping to make it drop the baby. But the effort failed and Anne-Marie watched helplessly as the bird carried her baby off into the clear blue sky. The body of the youngster was never found.

○ ○ ○

Eagles are not usually dangerous to man. Even the largest, the golden eagle, is rarely more than a metre long, with a two-metre wingspan. They prey on rabbits, rodents and young wild goats. Though they usually avoid man whenever possible, eagles have

been known to attack people who approach their nests when eggs have been laid.

The bird which carried off Anne-Marie's baby was almost certainly a golden eagle which probably noticed the baby moving and dived down from the sky, mistaking it for a rodent or rabbit.

This child-snatching behaviour has been reported of a number of different animals. It seems that animals who would ordinarily avoid humans are quite likely to attack babies and children whenever they get the chance. Perhaps they recognize that adult humans can be dangerous adversaries, but that young children are fairly defenceless against attack.

One such animal is the cougar, or puma, which inhabits North America. This large cat is over two metres in length and has powerful legs and claws. It usually avoids humans, even hiding in trees when people are nearby, but will sometimes attack children. One frightening attack launched by a cougar occurred in Washington State in 1886.

Bob and Johnny Farnham had spent the day at the village school and were now walking back to their family farm two miles distant. Before setting out, twelve-year-old Johnny had spent some of his pocket money on a bottle of lemonade.

'Here,' he said to six-year-old Bob, 'you have a drink.' He passed the bottle to his brother who smiled.

'Thanks,' said Bob. He took a mouthful of lemonade and passed the bottle back to his brother. 'What'll we do when we get home?'

'Well,' said Johnny. 'First we must keep out of

Mum's way. If she sees us with nothing to do she'll give us a job.'

Bob nodded, remembering that he had spent most of the previous evening helping his mother with some sewing. He had been made to fetch and carry pieces of cloth and thread.

'Perhaps we could play by the creek,' he suggested.

'Perhaps,' replied Johnny. 'Or we could go over to the Johnstone place to see their baby foal. Mr Johnstone says it will grow up to be a strong plough horse like its mother.'

'Ooh look,' cried Bob. 'A butterfly.' The pretty insect fluttered across the road and settled on a dead tree branch lying by the roadside. Bob trotted across to look at the brightly coloured insect before it flew off again.

Johnny carried on walking. He took another mouthful of lemonade. The hot weather had lasted several days now and he was glad that he had thought to buy a drink before starting off home.

A loud snarling sound, followed by an ear-piercing scream shattered the calm of the forest and caused Johnny to spin around. A few feet away he could see his brother lying in the road with a cougar standing over him. Bob was screaming and had his arms over his head to try to protect himself.

Without even stopping to think of his own danger, Johnny rushed forwards shouting loudly. The cougar looked up and snarled, revealing its long sharp teeth. Johnny did not stop but ran up to the cougar, beating it over the head with the lemonade bottle.

With a savage growl the cougar lashed out with its claws, slashing through Johnny's shirt and cutting his chest. Again Johnny struck the animal with the lemonade bottle. The cougar started backwards, snarling fiercely, as the bottle slammed onto its snout. Bob scrambled to his feet and ran off down the road.

Johnny stood facing the cougar. The beast lunged again, slashing its claws deep into Johnny's leg, but the cougar did not press its attack. Robbed of its prey, the cat did not want to risk facing a larger human. With one last snarl it turned around and bounded off into the forest, leaving Johnny to run after his brother.

He caught up with Bob after a hundred yards and stopped him.

'Are you all right?' he gasped.

'I'm sore,' said Bob. He looked down at his front. His shirt was torn and his chest was bleeding. He burst into tears.

'Don't worry,' said Johnny soothingly. 'We're nearly home now and Mum will soon make you better!' The boys limped home and told their mother what had happened. She quickly bandaged their wounds and sent for the doctor. That afternoon the boys' father set off with a gun to track down the cougar, but he failed to find it.

o o o

Equally likely to take babies is the hyena, a powerfully built animal which lives in Africa and parts of Asia. The strength of the hyena has become legendary; it is able to drag heavy carcasses for long distances and can snap thick bones with its jaws. Hyenas gain most of their food by scavenging from kills made by lions or leopards, but will also hunt for themselves when hungry. Forming into packs, the hyenas are able to kill sheep, zebras and cattle. Lone hyenas have also been known to hunt, and it is these which pose the greatest threat to human children.

When, in the spring of 1958, Douglas Anderson decided to take his family on a holiday in South Africa's Kruger National Park, they were delighted. That weekend the family – Mary, Douglas and their two young children – drove out to the untamed savannah which made up the National Park. All day the tough four-wheel drive vehicle travelled along the dirt roads of the park until they reached a campsite.

Though it was some hours before dark, Douglas Anderson knew that the next site was many miles away, so he decided to pitch camp for the night. While the children played, Douglas and his wife erected the tent and collected firewood from the surrounding scrub. As the sun sank in the west a small coach pulled up. A dozen people got out. Soon they made friends with the group of people and decided to have a party together that evening.

It was nearly dark by the time the coach party had set up their tents. Douglas and Mary collected some more firewood, and built a fire large enough to cook everyone's food. The two boys, Terry and Andrew, were allowed to stay up beyond their normal bedtime, but eventually they became tired.

'Come on you two,' said Mary. 'It's time you went to bed.'

'Oh, Mum,' complained Andrew, the older of the two, 'can't I stay up a little longer?'

'Nope,' said his mother, 'we have to be up early in the morning and I don't want you being worn out.'

Once the boys were safely tucked up in bed Mary returned to the campfire to join her husband and their new friends. For some time the adults sat around talking. Douglas found that Harold, one of the coach party, did the same job as himself. They talked business while the others chatted.

Suddenly Mary heard a strange noise. It sounded like something between a bark and a grunt. She looked around, but could not see anything.

A piercing scream from the boys' tent shattered the silence of the night. Mary was on her feet in seconds, running towards her children. As she approached the tent, she saw a dark shape creep from the tent flap and drag something off into the night. Seconds later Andrew ran screaming out of the tent.

'It's got Terry,' he shouted. 'It's got Terry.'

Mary caught her son.'What do you mean,' she asked, trying to stay calm. 'What's got Terry?'

Andrew was sobbing with fright. 'I don't know,' he said. 'It was hairy and smelt horrible. It's got Terry.'

By this time the men had come up. One of them, Jim, had an electric torch in his hand.

'Did anyone see which way it went?' he asked.

'I saw something make off over there,' said Mary pointing in the direction she had seen the dark shape move.

'Come on then,' said Jim. 'Let's follow it.'

He strode off into the darkness, followed by Douglas, Harold and the others.

'Terry,' shouted Douglas. 'Terry, are you there?'

There was a whimper in reply.

'Over here,' shouted Douglas. 'I heard something.'

Jim came over with the torch. The whimper came again and Jim shone his torch in the direction of the noise. Lying on the ground was Terry, covered in blood.

Douglas rushed to him, picking the boy up in his arms. Quickly carrying him back to the camp, Douglas told Mary to fetch the first-aid kit from the car. In the light of the fire and lanterns, Douglas found that his son was not badly hurt, but that he had been bitten and scratched many times by a wild animal. Working quickly, Douglas bandaged the wounds.

The next day Douglas showed Andrew and Terry pictures of several different animals. When he showed them a picture of a hyena both boys said that was the animal which had attacked Terry during the night. The attack on Terry Anderson was a very unusual event. Hyenas in Kruger National Park had

never before been known to attack humans before
or since Terry was attacked.

O O O

Very different were the hyenas of Bhagalpur in
India. There a pack of hyenas managed to kill a
young girl and drag her into the jungle where they
ate her. Several days later they returned to Bhagalpur. This time they killed and ate a young baby.
These hyenas became skilled at creeping into houses
and killing children quickly and silently. In the
course of four weeks the hyenas killed and ate nine
children.

Eventually a team of armed police were given the
task of guarding the town. They shot some of the
hyenas and drove the rest away.

O O O

Not all attempts by wild animals to take young children end in tragedy. Sometimes the animals will take
children without the least intention of killing them.
One such curious case was discovered in India in
1920 when Joseph Singh received a strange piece of
news.

Joseph Singh ran a small mission station in the
village of Midnapore. He taught the local children
how to read and write and acted as a doctor to the

surrounding district. On 17th October some men from a neighbouring village came to see Singh.

'Good morning,' said Singh. 'How can I help you?' He thought perhaps that the men wanted to enrol a child from their village in his school.

'Please, Reverend Singh,' said one of the men, named Ranjit. 'There is a devil living in the forest near our village. We want you to drive it away.'

'There is no devil in the forest,' said Singh, who did not believe the superstitious tales of the villagers. 'Perhaps you have seen a tiger or a wolf.'

'Oh, no sir,' said Ranjit. 'The devil runs with the wolves, but it is not a wolf. It is a devil-man.'

Singh looked at the men before him and could tell that they weren't lying. They had obviously seen something in the forest which had frightened them and which they believed to be a devil. Of course, Singh did not believe that they had seen a devil at all, but some kind of animal. Still, he thought it best to set their minds at rest.

'All right,' he said. 'I shall come into the forest with you to see this devil.'

Singh picked up his walking stick and followed the men into the forest. Some five miles into the jungle, Ranjit turned and signalled Singh to be quiet.

'The devil lives beneath that tree,' said Ranjit. 'It comes out at dusk.'

'Then we shall wait for it,' said Singh.

Carefully the men hid in the surrounding bushes. Singh chose to lie beneath a bush from which he could see the base of the tree where the devil was supposed to live.

As the sun slowly dipped towards the western horizon a furry grey muzzle came out of a hole beneath the tree.

Singh looked at Ranjit and raised his eyebrows, asking if this was the devil. Ranjit shook his head. The muzzle showed itself to belong to a large she-wolf. Slowly the wolf climbed out of the hole and stood before the tree. It looked around and then gave a low yelp.

A small wolf cub scampered out of the hole, then a second. Singh watched the young animals playing together for a moment, then he gasped in surprise.

Clambering out of the hole was a creature which appeared to be a devil indeed. It looked like a human running on all fours, but with a huge, very hairy head. Seconds later a second 'devil' emerged and began playing with the wolf cubs.

Before Singh could stop them, Ranjit and the other men had dashed forwards and beaten the wolves to death with their clubs. Then they turned on the 'devils'.

'Stop,' shouted Singh, 'stop at once!'

The men hesitated before attacking the 'devils' and looked at Singh. Singh came running over and looked at the creatures which were cowering against the tree.

'These are not devils,' he said. 'They are children.'

The men looked again at the creatures and saw that they were indeed two little girls. They were aged about seven and what looked like large heads were simply massively tangled clumps of hair.

'What shall we do with them?' asked Ranjit.

'Give them to me,' said Singh. 'I shall look after them.'

Singh took the wild children back to his mission. The girls were clearly human, but showed some animal characteristics. They were entirely unable to speak, but uttered strange howling and yapping sounds when they got excited. They were not interested in food such as vegetables or cooked meat, but when shown raw meat they would leap at it and devour it whole. Singh named the girls Amala and Kamala.

After a year Amala died, but Kamala survived. Over the following nine years she learnt to speak and to eat like a human. However, she still behaved like a wild animal and was thought to have a mental age of about three. She died at about the age of sixteen.

It would appear that the two girls had been snatched from their homes by the mother wolf when they were very young. The mother wolf had then cared for the girls, bringing them up as if they were wolf cubs. Only when the villagers reported the sightings to Singh did the girls come to the notice of civilization.

Stories such as this have been reported several times. In 1850 a wild boy was discovered living with wolves at Sekandra in India. He was captured by villagers and taken to an orphanage. Like Amala and Kamala he refused vegetables and was unable to speak. After a few months the boy fled from the orphanage and ran back to the jungle. He was never seen again.

More recently, in 1973, a boy was found in Sri Lanka who had been living with a troop of monkeys. He couldn't talk, but could climb trees expertly.

It would seem that not all children taken by wild animals are killed for food.

THE JUNGLE HUNTERS

Tigers are the most powerful hunters in Asia, growing to a length of over three metres. There are various types, or sub-species, of tiger, each of which lives in a particular area. The Siberian tiger is the largest, measuring over four metres long, while the smallest is the slender Javan tiger, usually well under three metres in length.

All types of tigers are extremely powerful beasts, well able to kill any other animal in the forests where they live. For thousands of years the tiger roamed Asia fearing no other animal, not even man. But during the past two centuries the tiger has become seriously threatened. Modern guns and traps have been used to kill thousands of tigers, while the felling of the forest has denied them a safe home. In India, which once had a tiger population of around 60,000, less than 2,000 survive. These animals are carefully preserved by a Government programme known as Project Tiger.

The vast majority of tigers are afraid of humans and avoid contact with them whenever possible. They are usually content to eat deer, wild pigs and other animals, but sometimes a tiger will turn into a maneater. This may happen when a tiger is wounded or crippled and is unable to catch its usual prey, but some tigers turn maneater for no obvious reason. When a tiger turns maneater a terrible and voracious

> **killer is let loose on the human population of the area. Fear spreads through the land and few people venture out after dark. One of the most horrific encounters with a maneater was that of the newly married Gunta couple who lived in a village near the tea-growing region of Nilgiri in eastern India about sixty years ago.**

One day a tinker arrived in the village to sell his goods, but he brought news far more interesting than any of his pots and pans.

'Poor Ahmed the cattle herder was killed at Mapani five days ago,' he told the anxious villagers. 'The boy helping him saw the tiger drag Ahmed into the jungle. And now people think the tiger killed Rajesh.'

'You mean that old man who went to Jaipur?' asked Gunta. 'We thought he had decided to stay on with his cousin for a few days.'

'Oh no,' replied the tinker, 'he left Jaipur three weeks ago but did not reach home. I say the tiger got him.'

After that the villagers decided to take no chances. A letter was written to the British Inspector asking for a hunter to come to kill the tiger. Meanwhile, nobody worked alone in the fields nor did anyone venture out of doors at night. Once darkness fell, doors and window shutters were locked and barred. The villagers felt safe behind locked doors, but as events proved they were far from being secure.

Five days after the tinker visited the village, the Guntas retired for the night as usual. They had little reason to suspect they were about to undergo the most terrible and tragic ordeal of their lives. About three o'clock in the morning the husband awoke with a start. At first he could not think what had disturbed him. Then a faint noise came from outside. Thinking one of his neighbours had been brave enough to go to tend the cattle, Gunta opened the shutters of his window to offer help.

Instead of a neighbour, Gunta was shocked to see a large tiger barely four paces away. As soon as the tiger realized it had been seen, it froze. For several seconds man and tiger stared at each other, neither daring to move. Then Gunta slowly closed the shutters and retreated to his bed.

Gunta knew tigers rarely entered villages and guessed the intruder might be the maneater, but he comforted himself with the thought that the doors and windows were securely locked. Anyway, he reasoned, the tiger might not be the maneater, but another tiger after one of the cattle.

Gunta was not left in doubt about the tiger's intentions for long for after only a few seconds he heard the tiger snuffling around the walls of the hut. The beast circled the little building twice, sniffing and scenting the air. Once or twice it grunted in satisfaction as it caught the scent of humans.

When the tiger reached the door, it stopped and silence fell again. Gunta began to hope that the beast had left when it could not find a way into the hut, but then he heard the tiger grunt on the other side of the door. Then there was a creaking sound as the animal pushed against the door, trying to get in. The door held, but the tiger tried again. Gunta's fear turned to terror as the door groaned under the strain.

The squeaking timbers woke up Gunta's wife.

'What's going on?' she asked.

'Shh,' hissed Gunta, 'there's a tiger outside. It's by the door.'

Gunta's wife caught her breath, listening to the heavy breathing of the hunter. 'What shall we do?' she asked.

'There's not much we can do,' replied Gunta. We haven't got a gun and my harvesting knife won't be much good. All we can do is hope it goes away. Let's stay quiet.'

A third time the tiger pushed against the door and this time one of the planks gave way and the tiger managed to get a paw inside the hut. Gunta shrank back and his wife gave a short scream of fear. Hearing this the tiger seemed to go mad. It roared loudly, shattering the tense silence. Retreating from the door, the tiger sprang forwards throwing its entire weight onto the timbers. With a loud crack, another plank gave way. Thoroughly maddened, the tiger snarled and roared and as it clawed at the shattered wood, each blow enlarging the hole in the door. The Guntas were paralysed with fear. There seemed to be no escape.

With a final powerful blow, the tiger demolished the door in a shower of splinters. Quaking with fright, Gunta bravely stepped forwards with his knife, but the tiger simply brushed him aside with one swipe of its paw. Bruised and cut, Gunta was slammed backwards against the wall. The enraged tiger rushed past him and seized the woman in its powerful jaws, killing her in seconds. With a final growl, the tiger turned and dragged its victim out into the darkness. Gunta was left battered and bleeding within the wreck of his home. His wife's body was never found.

o o o

Tigers which have so lost their fear of humans as to raid villages are extremely rare. Such attacks have been reported only a few times this century, and the tigers which were responsible have always been caught or shot soon afterwards. Because these tigers are no longer afraid of man they do not flee as normal tigers would. Instead they actually try to hunt the man sent to kill them. Invariably the man with the rifle wins the battle and the maneater dies.

Most maneaters are more cunning and have careers which last far longer, sometimes for several years. Instead of entering villages, these beasts lurk by jungle tracks or forest paths, hoping to kill lone travellers. They remain wary of groups of people and even of humans who do not seem to be afraid. It is almost as if the tiger can sense when a tiger hunter is after him. This type of maneater will attack a farmer, but rarely attempt to kill a hunter. One of the most notorious of these maneaters was the Chowgarh tiger which prowled the jungles of the

Siwalik Hills during the 1920s and killed dozens of people.

This tiger turned maneater when it was a healthy young animal. It would appear that when tackling a porcupine, the beast's front paw was badly cut by the porcupine needles. For several days the tiger was unable to hunt properly and it became extremely hungry.

Eventually, a woman came across the tiger as it lay nursing its wounds. In anger and surprise the tiger slashed with its claws and killed the woman. It then ate some of her body and acquired a taste for human flesh which meant that it was never satisfied with deer and pig again. The tiger continued to attack humans occasionally.

Perhaps the most dramatic incident in the long and frightening career of the Chowgarh tiger began when a group of women left the village of Lohali to collect firewood. They walked about a mile from the village to where a patch of woodland ran along the top of a steep grassy slope which ran down to a turbulent mountain stream. One of the women, named Janoo, moved away from her companions to collect some larger pieces of wood along the edge of the steep slope.

When Janoo heard a slight rustling sound, she turned to see a pair of bright yellow eyes staring at her from beside a thorn bush. Seconds later the eyes moved forward, and Janoo saw they belonged to a large tiger. Janoo hardly had any time to react before the tiger sprang. Instinctively Janoo flung herself

backwards, forgetting how close to the edge of the near vertical slope she was.

Empty air was all that met Janoo's feet as she tumbled backwards through space. The horrified women saw the tiger arcing through the air after her. Then, with a terrific thud Janoo struck the ground, the blow knocking the air from her lungs and tumbling her on down the slope.

It was this which saved her life.

The flying tiger crashed into the long grass at the exact spot where the woman had first landed. It tried to spring again, but missed its footing on the steep slope and slid downhill on its haunches, snarling and roaring as loudly as it could. The struggling tiger crashed into Janoo, knocking her further down the slope, and slashed at her with its claws, carving a great gash across her back.

Still rolling down the hill Janoo was struggling for breath when she collided with a small bush. Her headlong fall was stopped, but the tiger missed the bush and went slithering on.

Janoo watched the tiger as it rolled over and over, snarling and clawing at the air until it splashed into the stream far below. Moments later the animal emerged from the far side of the stream. It shook itself dry and turned to gaze up the slope towards Janoo. It snarled, roared and then strode off into the forest.

Janoo, caught in the branches of the bush, felt her back hurting terribly. She crawled from the bush and began the long, painful journey back up the hill. Janoo had fallen about 100 metres when she struck the bush and she had to clamber the whole way on her hands and knees with the wound in her back causing her agony. When she reached the crest of the hill, Janoo found that the other women had run away, so she had to crawl all the way back to the village before she could receive help of any kind.

The British government, which then ruled India, offered a large payment for the killing of the Chowgarh tiger and many sportsmen tried to claim the prize. They set out buffalo as bait for the tiger, but none of them succeeded in killing the predator. It was as if the beast knew when a man with a gun was nearby and avoided all types of bait and trap. Eventually, early in 1929, the famous hunter Colonel Jim Corbett decided to try his skill.

For long periods of time, spread over an entire year, Corbett tried to track down the maneater, but he failed and the killings continued. In all the Chowgarh tiger killed at least sixty-four people, and probably more than forty others who vanished in the jungle without any explanation.

Finally, on 11th April 1930, Corbett visited the site of a recent kill and staked out a buffalo. He hoped the tiger would return that night and kill the buffalo so that he could ambush it the following evening.

Leaving the buffalo tied up in a field, Corbett started to walk back to the village where he was staying along a route which took him along a narrow rocky ravine in the heart of dense jungle. As Corbett rounded a corner in the gully, he suddenly found himself staring straight at the maneater. The tiger

was just two metres from him and was staring at him
with unblinking yellow eyes.

Corbett froze. He knew that any sudden movement would make the tiger spring. Slowly he lifted
his rifle, knowing that the movement had to be
steady and gradual if he was to survive. For long
seconds the tiger and the man stood staring at each
other as the gun gradually came round.

Corbett found that he had to hold the heavy gun
in his hand at full stretch and the weight became
increasingly hard to bear. It felt as if his arm was
about to give way. Eventually the barrel came up in
line with the tiger's chest. Bracing the gun against
his shoulder, Corbett fired. The gun roared, but the
tiger did not move. For an awful moment, Corbett
thought he had missed, but then the tiger slid slowly
to the ground. The bullet had penetrated its heart.

DEATH BY SUFFOCATION

There are many snakes in the world which are dangerous to man. The dreaded rattlesnake of North America has a bite poisonous enough to kill a man. Fortunately this snake usually sounds its rattle before striking, giving anyone who encounters it time to escape. More dangerous still is the silent taipan snake which lives in northeastern Australia. Each individual snake of this species has enough poison to kill over a thousand humans

Fortunately for humans, these venomous snakes are not maneaters. Snakes cannot bite flesh from victims, but must swallow prey whole and because these venomous snakes are too small to eat a man, they cannot become maneaters. But there are some snakes which are able to swallow humans – these are the giant crushing snakes which live in tropical areas of the world.

The Indian python and South American anaconda are among the largest crushing snakes. They are not poisonous, like their smaller cousins, but rely on muscle power to subdue their prey. When they catch a victim, the snakes wind their bodies around the quarry and squeeze. Slowly the breath is forced out of the prey and it eventually dies of suffocation. Once the animal is dead, the snake releases its grip and swallows its kill.

Naturally the size of prey which a crushing snake can eat depends entirely on its own size. Small snakes

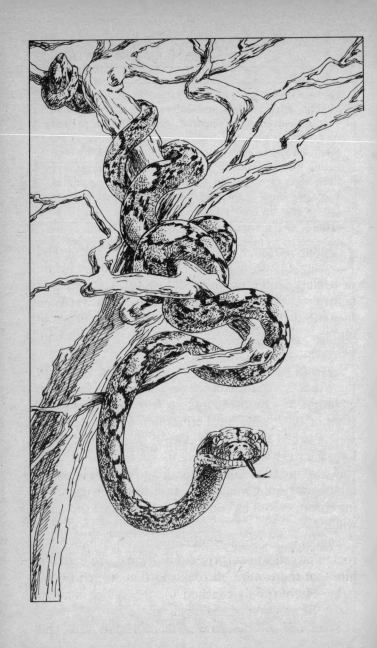

eat small prey, such as mice; larger snakes eat larger victims, such as pigs and calves. The largest snake ever measured by a scientist was an Indian python measuring ten metres. Anacondas reach similar sizes. Such creatures are quite capable of attacking and eating humans, but other, much larger snakes have been seen or captured from time to time, some of them so huge that they resemble monsters from horror movies rather than real animals.

Colonel Percy Fawcett opened his notebook and leaned back in his seat. He inspected the beetle in a glass jar before him. It was of a type never before recorded by a scientist and Fawcett was keen to write down an accurate description. In front of him the crew he had hired paddled the boat through the water.

Fawcett was exploring the remote Rio Negro in the Amazon rainforest on behalf of the Brazilian government. Before Fawcett travelled down the river in 1907, only local tribesmen had passed that way. Fawcett's job was to draw a map showing how long the river was and where its course ran. Fawcett was working hard in the sticky heat of the rainforest, taking measurements of the river and the surrounding forest as well as collecting examples of the local wildlife.

Suddenly the boat shuddered as if it had hit a rock. Fawcett was surprised. His local guide had told him that there were no rocks on that stretch of the river. He hurriedly reached for the sketch map to mark the position of the obstacle.

Then one of the rowers leapt to his feet and

screamed. At once all the rowers stopped work and began shaking with fright. Fawcett jumped to his feet to see what was happening. Everyone in the boat was shouting and screaming as the boat rocked violently to one side. Some of the men tried to row the boat backwards.

'What is it?' shouted Fawcett.

Pedro, Fawcett's translator, turned and pointed into the river.

'A giant snake,' he said. 'Shoot it, Colonel, shoot it.'

Fawcett glanced into the river and got the greatest surprise of his life. Swimming through the water was a snake far larger than the canoe in which he was travelling. Its triangular head alone was over a metre across.

Again the whole boat shook and rolled as the snake's body struck against it. The massive creature was moving away from the boat and began climbing out of the river on to the bank. It reared its head up and stared back at the speechless Fawcett and his terrified crew.

Thinking that the monster was about to attack them, Fawcett sprang into action grabbing his rifle, and pushing a bullet into the chamber. Raising the gun hurriedly to his shoulder, Fawcett took aim and fired. The bullet slammed into the snake's neck. With a violent spasm, the snake thrashed around, throwing up waves which threatened to overturn the boat. Then it shuddered along its whole length and lay still.

Fawcett sank back into his seat, realizing for the

first time just how frightened he had been. 'Pull over to the bank, Pedro,' instructed Fawcett.

'Yes, Señor,' replied Pedro, giving the necessary instructions to the men. The boat glided across to come to rest beside the huge body.

Fawcett stepped out and gazed at the snake. He found that the part of the snake on land was fourteen paces long and at least half as much again lay in the river. He was staggered by the sheer size of the animal.

'What is this thing?' asked Fawcett.

'I do not know, Señor,' said Pedro. He turned to the men and asked them something in their own language. One of the men became very excited and talked quickly. When he had finished Pedro turned to Fawcett.

'This man says that the monster is a sucuriju. He says that these animals live in the forest and are very dangerous.'

'I've never seen such a large snake,' said Fawcett. 'Ask him if they are common.'

Pedro spoke to the man and then translated his answer for Fawcett.

'He says that the animals are very rare, but that this is quite a small one. Other sucuriju are twice as big as this.'

Fawcett gazed at the huge reptile at his feet. He found it difficult to imagine a snake twice as big as this one. Such a creature would be nearly forty metres long.

The snake shot by Fawcett remains the largest ever measured by a reliable witness. Locals in the

Amazon rainforest sometimes report sighting animals up to forty-five metres in length, but these descriptions are impossible to verify. Such monsters as that shot by Fawcett and reported by the Indians would clearly be capable of killing and eating a human being.

○ ○ ○

One boy unlucky enough to appreciate the power of the python, a snake common in tropical Asia, was Tinto, a fourteen-year-old Malaysian boy. Tinto lived on Salebabu, an island in the Taland group off the Malaysian coast. As evening drew on one day in 1927 Tinto left his little village to visit some relatives a short distance away.

At first his route took him across paddy fields, filled with growing rice. Tinto strolled unhurriedly across the open ground, watching the vivid red sunset which filled the western sky. The path then climbed from the damp fields over a hill blanketed in dense jungle.

Tinto had travelled this way many times before and had never experienced any trouble. He strolled into the jungle, picking up a long stick which he tossed in the air and caught as he walked. He should be at his uncle's house in the next village within half an hour, he thought, in plenty of time for supper.

Passing a clump of vegetation, Tinto heard a sudden rustling. Spinning round, Tinto saw a snake at least five metres long racing across the forest floor towards him. Before he had time to move, Tinto felt his leg clamped in the terrifying grip of the creature's jaws.

Twisting its body violently to one side, the snake threw Tinto from his feet. A coil of snake slipped around his legs and caught hold. A second coil snapped around his waist. Tinto struggled desperately, shouting his alarm, but no answering shout came.

Using his stick, Tinto beat on the snake's gleaming flank, but if the snake felt the blow it took no notice. Throwing the stick aside, Tinto prised his fingers under the coil around his waist and strained to push it clear. To his horror a fresh coil appeared and wound around his chest.

The snake began to squeeze. Tinto pushed with his arms, but the snake did not shift its position. Tinto gasped for breath, and the snake began to squeeze tighter.

Tinto screamed, and the snake tightened its grip. Almost sobbing with the effort of breathing, the boy thumped his hands against the snake. The cold reptile simply exerted more pressure, crushing the air from the boy's lungs.

After a few spasmodic movements, Tinto lay still. He was dead. The snake continued to squeeze for a while, until it was certain the boy was no longer alive, then it relaxed its grip. Sliding from the still body of the boy, the snake sniffed its prey. Gliding slowly through the leaves which carpeted the ground, the snake shifted its position around to the head of the boy.

Opening its jaws the snake took the boy's head and shoulders between its teeth and began to swallow.

At that moment a man came running round the curve in the path. He had heard Tinto screaming and had come to help. In his hand the man carried an axe for he had been chopping firewood in the jungle. Taking in the situation at a glance the man ran forwards and struck the snake with the axe. The blow cut deep into the reptile, which thrashed about violently until a second hack from the axe finished it off. The man dragged Tinto from the snake's mouth and recognized him at once. Picking up the body he carried it to Tinto's village for burial.

○ ○ ○

The snake which attacked Tinto clearly saw him as prey and intended to eat him. The same is probably not true of the python which struck Tinkosa Ngurta in 1975.

Tinkosa worked as a gardener in Durban, South Africa. On the morning of 25th February Tinkosa visited the Jackson home. He always worked in the Jacksons' garden on Tuesdays and was largely left to sort out the work himself. That was the way Tinkosa liked it because he could decide what work to do and when to do it. That was better than being told exactly what to do, as happened with some of his customers.

The previous week Tinkosa had noticed that the

garden hedge needed trimming, so he decided to tackle that job first. Picking up his shears, Tinkosa strolled over to one end of the hedge. It was a long hedge and it would probably take most of the morning to trim it neatly into shape. Tinkosa rolled up the sleeves of his overalls and set to work.

By mid-morning Tinkosa was doing well. He had reached the large tree which overhung the far end of the hedge. He would be finished well before noon, and would then be able to get on with some other jobs.

Suddenly Tinkosa felt a heavy weight fall on his shoulders from the tree and heard a loud hissing. Something clamped itself around his waist so tightly that he gasped for breath. Dropping his shears in alarm, Tinkosa grabbed for his waist, and instantly felt a cold, rough object tighten around his neck. Screaming in fright, Tinkosa grabbed at his throat. The rough object felt round and hard.

A snake's head drifted into sight in front of Tinkosa's startled eyes. Desperately he lunged at the head with his hand, but the snake's supple neck whipped its head out of reach. The coil around Tinkosa's neck was tightening. He could almost feel his throat being crushed. As Tinkosa choked for breath he saw the lady from next door walk out of her back door. Tinkosa waved, desperately hoping that she would see him. The old lady took one look at him, screamed and dashed back indoors.

The pain in his neck becoming almost unbearable, Tinkosa made another grab at the snake's head, but missed again. His waist felt as if it had an enormously strong piece of elastic stretched around it, but his throat felt as if it was about to collapse under the pressure. His face felt hot and flushed as the blood in his head rushed to the skin. Gripping the snake desperately, Tinkosa wrenched at it, clawing with his fingers.

Suddenly he was free. Collapsing to the ground, he fought for breath. Air rushed into his lungs, roaring painfully past his raw throat. As he lay doubled up, Tinkosa saw the snake which had nearly killed him glide away into a bush.

Moments later a police car screamed up and two men jumped out. They ran over to Tinkosa.

'Are you OK?' one of them asked. 'The lady next door phoned us to say you were being attacked by a snake.'

Tinkosa nodded, gasping for breath. 'Yeah,' he panted. 'It's over there, in that bush.'

One policeman advanced on the bush while the second covered him with a pistol. Thrashing the bush with a stick, the policeman drove the snake from cover. It dashed across the lawn towards a shrubbery.

Tinkosa watched it in surprise. The creature was barely two metres long. Tinkosa was staggered that such a snake would have attacked him. It certainly could not have eaten him for snakes can only swallow prey whole, and are incapable of taking bites of flesh. Perhaps the snake had felt threatened in some way, or had mistaken Tinkosa for a smaller animal.

In fact attacks of large constricting snakes on humans are very rare. Man is not a normal prey of such animals. When a person is attacked it may be that the snake, taken by surprise, mistakes the human for another creature. The reasons why the python attacked Tinto, the Malaysian boy, are unclear, though it is possible that he disturbed the snake in some way.

Far more people are killed each year by the bites of poisonous snakes than are eaten by constricting snakes. Strictly speaking the deaths from venomous snakebites do not come under the subject of maneating. The snakes involved are far too small to eat a human; often they are less than one metre long.

Poisonous snakes only strike at a human if they feel threatened. If a person treads on a snake when walking through long grass, for instance, the snake is liable to bite. Different snake bites work in different ways. Some are so poisonous that they will kill a person in seconds. Others may take many hours to have effect and many are no more dangerous than a mosquito bite. This is because snake venom is not designed to kill people. It is usually used to kill animals around the size of a rabbit on which the snake preys. The snake will only bite a large animal, such as a human, in defence.

It is impossible to say how many people die of snake bites each year, because many deaths occur in remote areas where proper records are not kept. However, we do know that on average some fifteen people die each year in the United States, while a similarly small number of victims die in Australia. Most of these deaths occur in the southern states of the USA where the highly venomous diamondback and cottonmouth snakes are more common. In Sri Lanka about 800 people die each year. The number of deaths is so great because the island is inhabited by the dangerous common krait snake and because the people usually walk barefoot.

The only venomous snake in Britain, the viper or adder, is not very poisonous. Even if a person is bitten by this snake it is unlikely that they will die but they must get to a hospital fairly quickly. On average one person dies every ten years from a snake-bite in Britain.

GIANTS OF THE OCEAN

Whales are the largest and most impressive animals in the world. The biggest whale is the blue whale, which is found in all the oceans of the world. This huge animal can grow to over thirty metres in length and weigh over 140 tons. It cruises slowly through the oceans, feeding on countless millions of tiny animals known as krill, straining the small organisms from the water with a special filter in its mouth. Most of the large species of whale, including the twenty-metre sei and nineteen-metre humpback, feed in this way. The twenty-metre sperm whale, however, has teeth and feeds on squid. Smaller species tend to hunt fish, seals and other marine animals.

In recent years many species of whale have come close to extinction, due to the hunting activities of man. Whale bodies contain various substances, such as oil and ambergris, which man finds useful for various industrial purposes. The increasing demand for these substances has led to greater numbers of whales being hunted. From the 1920s onwards so many whales were being killed that the remaining whales could not breed fast enough to replace them and total numbers fell.

The International Whaling Commission was set up by several countries to control the numbers caught to manageable levels. However, some countries refused to join and others ignored instructions. The hunting of whales still continues to threaten the sur-

vival of several species of whale, including the largest
of all, the blue whale.

Whales could pose a threat to man by their very
size. Any human swimmer struck by a whale's tail
would stand little chance of survival, and several
men have suffered such a fate. However, there are
numerous reports of whales which actively intend to
kill humans and even to eat them. Most of these
reports come from many years ago, when whales
were more numerous and ships were smaller, but
some reports come from the present day.

In the 1270s an Italian named Marco Polo left
home to travel across Asia to the court of the
great Chinese Emperor Kublai Khan in Peking. He
was the first European to complete the dangerous
journey and to record what happened to him and
what he found. When passing through the area now
known as Iran, Marco Polo spoke to many sea captains who sailed the Indian ocean. From them he
learnt of the dangers of the sea, and one of the
captains told him a particularly terrifying story about
an encounter with a whale.

Abdul Hamid, the captain of a cargo ship left his
home port of Masqat bound for Calicut in India. A
few days after the voyage began, Abdul noticed that
trouble was brewing among the crew.

When he asked one of the sailors, Ajiz, to hand
over a long dagger he was carrying, Ajiz turned on
him and tried to plunge the knife in the captain's
chest. Two other men drew out knives and were
threatening to attack Abdul, whilst the other men
went to his rescue. Soon all the sailors on board

were involved in the fighting. Suddenly the whole ship shuddered, causing Abdul to lose his balance and crash heavily on to the deck. Grasping on to a rope for support, Abdul felt the deck shake and lurch sideways. Then the deck lay still.

Abdul leapt to his feet and looked around. He could not imagine what had happened. They were many miles from land in the middle of the ocean and would not reach any large rocks or reefs for several days. The deck was at an angle which was steepening with each second. They had obviously hit something, and the ship was sinking . . .

'Abandon ship!' shouted Abdul. He made for the small boat which was lashed to the deck by the rear mast and began to undo the ropes which held it in place.

But he had forgotten Ajiz. Searing pain struck through Abdul's back as the mutineer stabbed him with his knife. Abdul spun round, staring into the angry eyes of Ajiz. The knife swung back, ready to deliver the death blow. Then Ajiz was gone, knocked sideways by a heavy blow from Majid, the second-in-command.

'Come on, Majid,' said Abdul. 'Help me launch this boat, or we are dead.'

Other members of the crew helped untie the knots. As Abdul leant back against the mast he noticed the whale he had seen earlier surfacing barely a hundred paces from the ship. As he watched the whale turned, gathered speed and headed straight for the ship. Suddenly Abdul realized that the ship was being attacked by the whale.

Abdul gave a shout of alarm as he watched the giant creature thundering towards him. The great black body was gaining speed with every second, aiming its bulk at the centre of the ship. Now it was barely forty metres away.

Now twenty.

Now ten.

There were screams as the massive whale slammed into the ship. Planks caved in, splinters flew through the air and the green sea cascaded over the deck. The foaming waters were rushing into the hole and the ship was sinking fast.

Abdul felt himself being dragged up and backwards by the scruff of his neck and found himself lying in the bottom of the small boat, surrounded by the crew.

From the lifeboat Abdul saw the ship slide gracefully beneath the waves. The whale surfaced nearby and spouted, sending its column of spray high into the air.

'Help, help,' called a faint voice.

Abdul looked in the direction of the voice to see Ajiz clinging to a broken plank. He was waving at them.

'Should we turn back back to help him?' asked one of the crew members.

Abdul was about to answer when the whale surfaced again. It rushed through the wreckage, throwing up huge amounts of spray as it passed. Then it

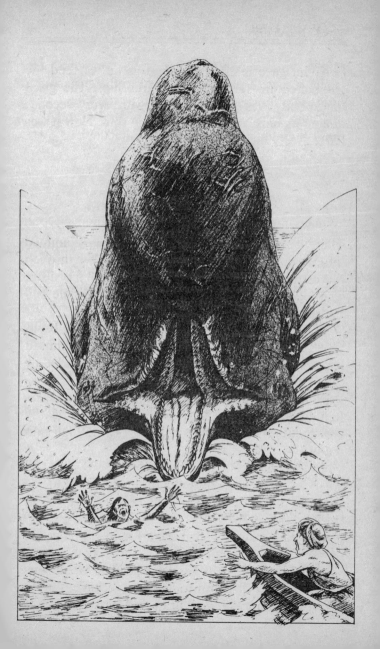

dived from sight. Ajiz was gone. Moments later some pieces of planking bobbed to the surface, but there was no sign of Ajiz. For three days Abdul and his men rowed their boat across the Arabian sea until they touched the shore at Karachi.

○ ○ ○

Whales are now much rarer in the Indian Ocean than during Abdul's time and dhows have not been attacked for many years. But whales are still active attackers of human craft, as a yachtsman named David Sellings found out to his cost in 1988.

In June of that year Sellings was taking part in a yacht race across the Atlantic Ocean. He was sailing alone, for the rules of the race allowed only one person in each craft. Sellings did not have time to become bored, however, for the needs of the yacht kept him almost continuously busy.

For several days after he left America Sellings encountered good weather. There was a fairly strong wind one day, but the waves had not grown large enough to cause him any worries. His yacht was strongly built with substantial sails and Sellings was confident that his craft could withstand any danger which the sea could throw at it, short of a full-scale hurricane. He was to be proved very wrong before the sun set on 17th June.

The day dawned bright and blustery with the sun shining down brilliantly on a sea whipped into a mass of short waves by a brisk breeze. After making adjustments to his rigging and sails, Sellings settled down at the stern of the yacht and turned the radio on. So long as the wind remained steady he would not have to alter the rigging and could concentrate on steering.

Sellings wondered how the other yachts in the race were getting on. He had lost sight of them the previous day as each man took a slightly different route to take advantage of what he thought to be better winds. Now Sellings was alone on the broad empty ocean.

Or so he thought.

As the yacht raced along, Sellings saw a dark shape breaking through the water surface. He glanced idly at the newcomer to see what it was. The shape had gone, but soon it returned. The black-and-white markings of the large barrel-shaped body were striking and distinctive. Selling recognized it at once as a killer whale, or orca.

Sellings knew these creatures were ferocious hunters of the ocean, preying on seals, dolphins, fish and penguins and that they often hunted in packs. Sellings guessed that the killer whale was not alone, and he was right.

Seconds later a second killer whale broke the surface. It swam beside the first for a few seconds, then dived from sight. A third and fourth whale appeared some distance away.

One killer whale, larger than the rest, surfaced quite close to the yacht and swam alongside. Sellings guessed that it must be about ten metres in length.

He had not realized that the killer whales were such large animals.

Something about the whale worried Sellings. It was swimming with its large, black eye above the surface of the sea, as if it were watching him. Sellings gazed back at the whale. He stood up and instantly the whale dived from sight.

Seconds later it surfaced again, continuing to stare at Sellings with its black eye. Looking around Sellings saw the sea being broken by at least a dozen whales as they swam in a pack some distance away. The whales were keeping pace with the yacht, neither falling behind nor overtaking it.

Sellings reached for his radio transmitter. Then he paused. He couldn't send out a distress message just because a whale was looking at him! The emergency services had more important things to do, and he did not want to appear silly. He replaced the microphone.

At that moment the large whale veered off, swimming off to join the rest of the pack two hundred metres away. Sellings heaved a sigh of relief. He had not liked the way the whale had been watching him. He hoped that he would not meet any more killer whales in the course of his voyage.

Then Sellings froze in terror. The whale was back, but it was not alone. The large killer whale was cruising a few metres from the port bow of the yacht. Other whales were swimming off the port quarter, following up the yacht. Sellings spun round in alarm. More whales were following on the starboard side of the craft.

As he watched the whales slowly spread out almost to encircle his craft. No matter which way he tried to turn he would find himself running into killer whales. Only the route straight ahead was open. It was as if the creatures were trying to shepherd him in a particular direction.

Sellings nestled back into his seat. He was worried, but comforted himself with the thought that he was safe on board his yacht. The killer whales would not be able to reach him there. The large whale swam close, racing along barely five metres away from where Sellings was sitting. It raised its head above the surface to gaze at Sellings with a hard, cold stare.

Then it was gone, diving beneath the surface. Sellings looked roundabout. The other whales were still there, cruising along around. They appeared threatening, but Sellings thought he was safe.

Suddenly his yacht lurched sideways and upwards as if it had been struck underneath by a terrific hammerblow. The sails shook loose in the breeze and the rigging rattled against the mast.

Sellings looked around in alarm. He could not imagine what had happened. The boat felt as if it had hit a rock, but he was thousands of miles from land. The yacht continued forwards as if nothing had happened.

The large whale surfaced once again. It raised its head above the water to gaze at Sellings, then dived from sight again. Long seconds of silence followed, broken only by the sound of the wind on the waves.

A terrific thud shuddered through the boat, shaking it from end to end. Sellings suddenly realized that the killer whale was attacking his yacht – it seemed to be ramming the craft from beneath.

The large whale reappeared beside Sellings. Then it veered off to one side and came thundering back. Sellings could scarcely believe the speed at which the whale was travelling. It sliced through the water like a powerboat, skimming beneath the surface with scarcely a ripple.

As the beast approached the yacht, Sellings braced himself. With a sickening crunching sound the whale struck amidships. Sellings was almost knocked from his seat by the blow. Scrambling to his feet, Sellings dashed forward. The side of the yacht was badly dented and he could see a few small cracks.

Sellings suddenly became worried about the previous attacks. He wondered if they had damaged the yacht at all. He strode to the entrance to the cabin. He could test the scale which told him if any water was collecting beneath the cabin floor.

As soon as he opened the door Sellings knew he was in serious trouble. Water was sloshing around the floor of the cabin. Another great shock slammed through the yacht as the whale struck again. A leak sprang in the wall of the cabin, water spurting in through the hole.

The yacht was sinking.

Sellings rushed back on deck. He was not certain how long the yacht would stay afloat, but if the whale continued its attacks on the craft it could not be for long. Sellings untied the emergency raft which was lashed to the deck of his ship.

The killer whale surfaced alongside the yacht, eyeing Sellings as he worked on the raft. Sellings glanced at the killer whale and shuddered. He had no doubt now that the whales were hunting him, trying to get him in the water so that they could eat him.

The yacht was doomed and Sellings knew that his only chance was to get aboard the raft before the boat sank. He also knew that he stood little chance of surviving. If the killer whales were able to sink a yacht they would have little difficulty smashing the small raft to pieces.

The bows of the yacht dipped into a wave, the water cascaded back along the deck, running into the cabin door. The craft was definitely lower in the water and it would not be long before it sank. Sellings glanced around at the whales. They were still keeping pace with the yacht.

Sellings scrambled aboard the raft, just as the yacht gave a final lurch and nosed beneath the waves. For a few seconds the yacht rested with its mast and sails showing above the sea. Then it slipped downwards beneath the waves.

Sellings was alone on the empty ocean, surrounded by the killer whales.

The large whale surfaced beside the raft, heaved its head out of the water and gazed at Sellings from a distance of just four metres. Sellings was convinced that within seconds he would be dead, eaten by a killer whale.

Instead the whale dived, followed by its companions, and never returned to trouble Sellings further. Sellings later got his emergency radio transmitter working and sent out a distress call and was picked up a few hours later by a passing ship. He was never able to understand why the whales did not return to finish him off, and experts were equally baffled. Some thought that the whales had not been attacking him at all, but Sellings was convinced of what he had seen. After all, his yacht had sunk.

○ ○ ○

It is known that packs of killer whales will attack much larger whales of other species, some up to twenty-five metres in length. It has been suggested that the killer whales might mistake yachts and other small ships for large whales. This would explain why the killer whales so often leave the humans alone once the ship has sunk. It is thought that the killer whales are continuing the attack on the boat beneath the surface of the water.

There can be no such mistake about the intentions of a pack of killer whales which attacked a man called Herbert Ponting in 1911. They were determined to eat him, and very nearly succeeded.

The incident occurred on the morning of 5th January, when the sun was emerging from a thick belt of cloud. Ponting climbed up on deck of *Terra Nova*, the ship on which he and his companions had been living for several weeks. They had sailed to Antarctica to study the wildlife and weather of the area and to make an attempt to be the first men to reach the South Pole. Ponting was a photographer whose task was to take pictures of everything which happened.

He looked at the sky, then turned to face the landscape behind the ship.

'Everything all right, Ponting?' asked the doctor.

Ponting turned to smile at Atkinson.

'Yes, Atch, fine,' he said, using the doctor's nickname. 'I was thinking that the light is just right for taking some pictures.'

Atkinson glanced up at the sky. 'I suppose it has been rather cloudy recently,' he remarked.

'Too true,' replied Ponting. 'And I need a good light when I'm working in these conditions. Cloudy days just aren't bright enough I'm afraid.'

Atkinson leant against the rail of the ship. 'You should be all right today though,' he said. 'Would you like a hand?'

Ponting grinned. 'I wouldn't mind,' he said. 'My equipment can be very heavy to carry around on the ice.'

The photographic equipment which Ponting had taken with him was of very high quality, but was rather old-fashioned. Ponting knew he could rely on his apparatus to take good photographs, but the large box cameras and bulky tripods weighed a great deal.

Ponting led Atkinson below and sorted out his equipment. He decided to take only one camera, but a selection of different lenses. Atkinson climbed up on deck as Ponting passed the boxes of equipment up to him.

'What type of pictures are you after?' asked Atkinson.

Ponting passed a box of lenses to his friend. 'I wanted to take some views of our camp,' he said. 'I've been concentrating on penguins and seals until now. It's about time I took some pictures of us and our home.'

'Good plan,' said Atkinson. 'The people back home in Britain will be keen to see how we survive in these sub-zero temperatures.'

The two men scrambled down from the ship to the snow-covered shore. Ponting was careful with his fragile equipment, which could be broken by the slightest accident.

'I think I might be able to get some good pictures from out on the ice,' said Ponting. 'Can you wait here for a moment before we go to the camp?'

'Of course,' said Atkinson. 'But don't be too long. It's freezing out here.'

'All right,' laughed Ponting and he trotted out beyond the ship on to the thick ice which covered the sea for more than two hundred metres from shore.

He passed a group of husky dogs, tied to a stake driven into the ice, and then turned to face the ship. The light was good, there could be little doubt about that, but the ship was blocking the view of the camp. He trotted a few metres to his left. That would be about right. He dropped a glove to mark the spot and began walking back towards Atkinson to help carry the gear out to take the photos.

Suddenly the ice in front of him lifted upwards

like a giant dome. The smooth surface cracked and shattered into dozens of pieces, the sea bursting through in great fountains of spray. The whole ice sheet shuddered with such violence that Ponting was thrown on to his back.

Ponting's first thought was that a massive explosion had blasted the ice apart. But he quickly realized that the team did not carry enough explosive for such a thing. Anyway, he reasoned, nobody would be so daft as to set off such an explosion.

Ponting picked himself up. The ice in front of him was shattered and broken to form a wide pool of water and ice fragments. A clear path of ice ran from his position to the shore to his right. Ponting moved in that direction.

'Are you all right?' shouted Atkinson across the gap.

'Fine,' said Ponting, 'but I don't know what's going on.'

With a resounding crack which could be heard for kilometres the ice heaved up again, smashing the path of solid ice and cutting Ponting off from land. Again he was thrown from his feet, but this time Ponting saw what was happening.

As the ice flew upwards, Ponting saw the unmistakable snouts of killer whales. The beasts had rammed the ice from beneath at high speed, smashing it to fragments. Even as the spray subsided, one of the whales surfaced in the hole they had caused, then dived again.

Looking round, Ponting realized that he was in trouble. The sheet of ice on which he was standing was now floating free, separated from the shore by open water dotted with pieces of ice.

The killer whales surfaced in numbers now. Ponting could see that there were at least a dozen of them, and he had the uncomfortable feeling that they were looking at him.

Some of the animals dived from sight and a few seconds later the ice not far from where Ponting was standing was struck from below. It shattered to pieces. Ponting found himself staring into the eyes and open jaws of a killer whale.

'Ponting,' shouted Atkinson, 'they're trying to get you in the water.'

'I know,' called back Ponting, worried by what was happening. 'Get the others, they might be able to help.'

Atkinson rushed to the ship, clambering on board and shouting for the other men to come out to the ice.

Ponting watched horrified as the whales grouped for another attack. When the creatures rammed the ice, they split the sheet in two, isolating Ponting on a piece barely thirty metres across. He knew that two more such attacks and he would be flung into the water and eaten alive.

Ponting glanced at the ship. He could see men climbing on deck. One of them had a rifle. Ponting looked back at the whales, realizing that his friends could not hope to reach him before the whales did. He decided to take a terrible risk to reach safety. Between him and the shore was a stretch of water perhaps twenty metres wide dotted with pieces of broken ice. Ponting guessed that some of the large pieces would support his weight.

Throwing a glance over his shoulder at the whales, Ponting sprinted forwards. As he reached the edge of the ice he leapt forwards, aiming for a large fragment of ice. His feet struck squarely, but slipped and flung him on to his back. Picking himself up, Ponting threw himself at another piece closer to shore. This time he nearly missed, his left leg slithering to the side and being plunged into the freezing water.

Ponting dragged himself upright again and looked around for another slab of ice. There was one! He leapt at it, landing securely. Even as he struggled for balance, Ponting heard a crunching sound; looking around he saw a large killer whale attacking the piece of ice he had just left.

Fear gripped Ponting as he realized how close to death he was. He leapt again, his boots skimming over the back of a whale as he did so. Another bound and he crashed on to the packed snow of the shore. Feeling the solid ground beneath his feet, Ponting collapsed and lay gasping on the ground. He was sweating despite the cold.

'Are you all right?' asked Atkinson as he ran up. 'Are you hurt?'

'I'm safe,' said Ponting. 'But I'm afraid that I'm a bit wet. And I left a glove out there.'

'Never mind the glove,' said Captain Scott, the team leader. 'You're safe, that's the main thing. Do you realize how close those devils got to eating you?'

Ponting sat up and nodded. 'I do, Captain,' he said with feeling. 'I most certainly do.'

o o o

The killer whales are acknowledged to be energetic hunters of the open ocean. They may attack humans whenever the opportunity presents itself, particularly if the whales are hungry or are led by an especially daring individual. The larger whales, however, are not generally reckoned to be maneaters. But, on occasions, they have been known to turn on humans and devour them.

In the last century men hunted whales by chasing them in rowing boats launched from large ships. At this time the whales often retaliated against their hunters. Sperm whales were especially aggressive and sank many whaling boats by ramming them or smashing them with their tails. On at least one occasion a whale even leapt out of the water to land on the whaling ship itself, nearly sinking the vessel.

Perhaps the strangest and most disturbing of these violent whaling incidents occurred in 1891 when the ship *Star of the East* was hunting whales off the Falkland Islands. When the unfortunate man at the centre of the incident reached home some months later he told his wife what had happened.

'It was early in February when it happened,' he said. 'We were cruising off the Falklands when the lookout shouted down to deck the traditional words for sighting a whale. "There she blows" he called.

'The captain rang the bell at once and we all ran up on deck. Within minutes the boats were being swung away and let down into the sea. I scrambled aboard my boat, alongside my old mate from school-days, Jim.

'The boatmaster told us to row like mad while the harpooner got himself ready in the bows. I pulled hard at my oar, Jim tugging hard at his. Glancing over my shoulder at the harpooner (Abraham, I think his name was), I saw he was carefully coiling the rope around in the base of the boat.

' "There she is" shouted the boatmaster pointing ahead of us. "Now row, boys" he said. "Row hard." We fair put our backs into it after that. The oars dipped in and out of the blue ocean, throwing up little fountains of spray at each stroke.

'Soon we began to catch up with the whale. It was a huge black sperm whale. As we approached it beat the water with its tail, throwing up a huge amount of spray and drenching us all to the skin. Then it dived below the surface. I thought we had lost it, but the boatmaster was an old hand at whaling. He told us where it would surface and got us to row to the spot.

'Sure enough the whale rose just where the boat-master had predicted. With a few powerful strokes at the oars we got the boat alongside and Abraham lifted the heavy harpoon in his hand.

'The sheer size of the whale was enough to frighten me, it was huge and was gliding through the water with immense power. Then Abraham flung the harpoon deep into the whale.

'The beast smacked the water with its tail, nearly overturning the boat, then dived from sight. At first the water churned where the whale had been, but this soon died down. There was absolute silence, except for the sound of the rope attached to the harpoon running out. When that stopped all I could hear was the quiet slapping of the water on the boat.

' "Hold tight, lads," said the boatmaster. "The whale is coming up again. Be ready to row when he surfaces."

'We sat at our oars waiting for a sign of the whale. The sea was calm and unbroken. Then it crashed to the surface in a fountain of spray and foam. Abraham began pulling in the rope as fast as he could, but he suddenly stopped and screamed. We all spun round, to see the whale powering towards us as fast as it could. I'll never forget the horror on the boatmaster's face as he watched that monster bearing down on us. The whale was so full of strength and anger that I never want to see such a thing again.

' "Pull" shouted the boatmaster. "Pull, quick." We needed no further urging and bent to our oars with a will. But it was no good, the angry whale was too quick for us. He came at us so fast that the sea was riding up in a wave in front of his head.

'I saw the boat strike this wave, and felt it heaving upwards. Then the whale struck us. The side of the boat caved in and I felt myself being tossed through the air. I struck the water with a terrific smack and sank beneath the surface.

'Suddenly there was a terrific roaring noise, like

the wind during a storm, and I was plunged into darkness. I felt as if something was pushing in on me from all sides and was carrying me forwards. I was pressed tight all around and was fighting for breath. Then I suddenly had more room.

'It was pitch black and I could not see a thing. I wondered if I had suddenly gone blind. It was very hot, far hotter than the hottest summer's day. I felt around me in the darkness. I was sitting in a great squidgy mass of something. It smelt horrible. It felt as if it was made up of hundreds of small pieces of something slimy. I reached out around me and felt something like a soft wall covered in slime.

'That was when I realized what had happened. I had been swallowed by the whale. I screamed in horror at the thought, but realized nobody could hear me. I knew that whales kept air in their stomachs as a sort of float to keep them bouyant in the water. That must be where I was. In the whale's stomach. The soft mass on which I was sitting was the chewed up pieces of fish and squid which the whale had eaten.

'I remember sitting there for a few minutes wondering what to do, realizing that there was nothing I could do. There was no way I could get out of the whale. Even if I did I would only drown. I was as good as dead, or so I thought. It was soon after that I fainted.

'The next thing I remember is having some cool water poured into my mouth. I opened my eyes to see a man bending over me. As soon as I looked up he sprang backwards and ran off. I sat up to find

myself in a small wooden cabin. Some pictures hung
on the wall and outside the windows I could see the
sea. I wondered what had happened. I remember
thinking that perhaps I had died and this was some
kind of after-life. It did not look like either Heaven
or Hell, though. It looked more like a ship's cabin
than anything else.

'I heard footsteps and the door opened. In walked
the captain of my ship. I was absolutely staggered
to see him.

' "Hello Bartley," he said. "You're feeling rather
better then?" I stared at him in surprise.

' "What happened?" I asked.

' "You were swallowed by the whale," he said.

' "I know," I replied, "I remember that. But how
did I get here?"

"Well," said the captain. "The day after you disappeared we caught up with the whale again and
killed it. As we were cutting up the carcass, to get
at the spermaceti and blubber, your mate Jim suggested cutting open the stomach to see if the whale
had swallowed you. We assumed you would be dead,
but we wanted to give you a decent burial. When
we cut open the stomach you were there all right,
but you were still breathing. It gave us quite a shock
I can tell you."

' "When was this?" I asked.

' "Over a week ago now," said the captain.
"You've been locked up in here ever since. You
were quite mad, you know, running around screaming and attacking anyone who came near you. We'd
just about given up any hope for you and I expected

to have to lock you up in a lunatic asylum when we got back to Great Yarmouth."

'So that's what happened,' concluded Bartley, 'I was swallowed by the whale, went mad and was rescued the following day, though there's some as say I'm still a little touched.' Bartley winked. 'I still have nightmares about the whole incident, but other than that I'm all right. I'll tell you one thing though. I'm never going whale hunting again!'

DEATH ON THE PLAINS

Lions are the great hunters of Africa. Powerful beasts weighing around two hundred kilos, they kill their prey with long sharp teeth and claws made to rip an animal apart.

Usually lions hunt in pairs or family groups, which are known as prides. They prefer to hunt at night, creeping up on a victim and then springing forwards with jaws agape. Sometimes prides of lions will chase prey over long distances, slowly tiring the victim out until it can offer little resistance to attack.

The prey of lions consists of the plant eaters which live on the savannah – these include giraffes, zebras and many different types of antelope. Lions usually run away from humans, knowing them to be dangerous, but some lions will suddenly become maneaters and appear to prefer eating humans to any other prey. Nobody knows why this happens, but when a lion turns maneater it becomes a voracious killer.

Until a few hundred years ago lions inhabited large areas outside Africa, including Greece, Persia and India. Over the years, however, the increasingly large numbers of humans in these areas has led to the disappearance of the lion. The people considered the lion to be a danger not only to themselves but also to cattle and sheep, so they hunted the lions to extinction.

Even in Africa the lion is now much rarer than it was only fifty years ago and has vanished from many

areas. Large National Parks in some African countries offer a safe home for lions as it is illegal to hunt
lions in these National Parks. It is perhaps ironic that
one of the largest National Parks is at Tsavo, where
two of the most famous and terrible maneating lions
once stalked their victims. The Tsavo lions became
world-famous, but their terrible career began very
quietly.

Colonel John Patterson sat back in his canvas
chair outside his tent and sipped his tea. He had
been given the job of supervising the building of a
railway across the savannah of Kenya, and the work
was being done very quickly.

He had three thousand men working for him, scattered in different camps along the railway. They had
laid many kilometres of track from Mombasa inland
without any serious difficulty. Patterson smiled,
hoping to get the railway finished within a few
months, finished his cup of tea and went to bed.

Patterson awoke suddenly to the sound of shouting and screaming. It was still dark. He hurriedly
pulled on his trousers and stepped out of his tent to
find a number of workmen running towards him
waving torches and lanterns and shouting loudly;
they seemed hysterical.

As the men approached they fell silent and one of
the foremen came forward.

'Oh, sir,' cried Mahina, tears running down his
cheeks. 'Ungan Singh is dead.'

'What?' exclaimed Patterson. Ungan was one of
his best foremen. He had travelled from India

specially to help with the bridge building. 'What on earth has happened? Was it an accident?'

'Oh no, sir,' wailed Mahina. 'He was killed by a lion.'

'A lion?' gasped Patterson.

'Yes, sir. I saw it myself. I share a tent with Ungan. I woke up in the middle of the night when Ungan screamed. There was a lion in the tent with us. It killed Ungan and dragged him outside.'

'That's right,' shouted some of the men. 'We saw the lion dragging Ungan off into the darkness.'

Patterson didn't like the sound of this. He felt sick, but was determined to find out what had happened. Mahina and the other men led Patterson to a tent on the edge of the camp. There were pools of blood around the tent and the footprints of a large lion in some sand nearby. Patterson looked at the tracks and then gazed into the darkness.

'We can't do much tonight,' he said. 'You try to sleep and I'll stay on guard with my gun. We'll try to find Ungan in the morning.'

When dawn came, Patterson gathered some of the men together and set off to follow the lion's tracks. They came to a patch of open, sandy ground where they found all that was left of Ungan Singh: some human bones and large pools of blood drying in the morning sun.

Patterson shuddered at the thought of a lion eating his foreman.

'Collect the bones so that we can bury them,' said Patterson. 'I'll try to track down the lion.'

The men placed the bones in a bag while Patterson

took his rifle and set off in search of the lion. He found that he was actually following the tracks of two lions, but he soon lost them on some stony ground. He walked back to the camp, deep in thought. He knew that lions usually hunted at night and feared that the lions might return the following evening.

When Patterson returned to the camp he told his men to stop work on the railway and start building a strong fence around the camp. The men cut down the thorny bushes which grew across the plains and wove the branches together to form a thick, dense fence over three metres tall. Patterson hoped that such a formidable barrier would keep the lions out of the camp. While the men were building the thorn fence, Patterson sent a man riding round the other camps to tell them about the lions and order them to build fences as well.

For the next three nights the lions did not attack.

'The thorn fences are keeping them out, sir,' said Mahina on the fourth day.

'Yes,' said Patterson, 'and they don't seem to hunt during the day.'

There was a sudden disturbance among the men working on the railway line nearby. Patterson glanced over and recognized the chief of the local Wa Jamousi tribe striding towards him.

'Hello Engomani,' hailed Patterson.

'Good morning, Mister Patterson,' said Engomani. 'I came to tell you that the lions have attacked my village and killed a woman.'

'When did this happen?' asked Patterson, glancing at Mahina.

'Last night,' replied Engomani, 'just as the moon rose above the hill.'

'Well, we've built these thorn fences around our camps,' said Patterson waving his arm at the structures. 'Perhaps you should build them around your village.'

Engomani looked at the thorn barrier and agreed to try it.

Two nights later the lions broke through the fence at an outlying camp and killed two men, dragging the bodies off into the night. The following night they returned and killed a third man. Patterson slept at the camp on the third night, with his rifle at the ready. The lions did not return, but attacked a different camp, dragging a foreman off to his death.

Patterson decided to spend the night at the camp which had just been attacked. As usual he slept with a loaded rifle by his side, but he had scarcely closed his eyes when one of the guards came running into his tent.

'The lions are here,' he gasped. 'I saw them in the moonlight outside the fence.'

Patterson grabbed his rifle and followed the man outside. The workman led Patterson to the thorn hedge. He pointed to a patch of grassland about fifty metres away.

'Over there,' he said.

Just then an ear-splitting scream rang out, shattering the quiet of the night. The sounds were coming from the far side of the camp. Patterson and the guard ran through the camp in the direction of the screams.

When they arrived at the scene, they found a man lying on the ground with a large wound in his leg, surrounded by a large pool of blood. Patterson took his shirt off and used it as a bandage on the wounded man.

'What happened?' he asked.

The wounded man winced with pain. Then he pointed beyond the thorn fence.

'Lions,' he gasped.

Patterson looked in the direction the man was pointing and caught a glimpse of a large lion dragging something into a patch of bushes. He grabbed his gun, but the lion was gone before he could fire a shot.

Other men had gathered round. The wounded man was in great pain, but he managed to tell Patterson that the lions had pushed their way through the fence and attacked him and another guard. The other man had been killed and dragged off, but the lions had left him alone after clawing his leg.

Finishing the bandaging, Patterson walked to the thorn bush and gazed into the night, straining his eyes to catch sight of the lions. Suddenly a loud roar boomed out. Patterson jumped, and some of the men ran to their tents. The roar came again and Patterson knew it was the lion feeding on the dead guard. The sounds seemed to be coming from the patch of bushes where he had seen the lion earlier.

Patterson aimed his rifle at the bushes and fired, hoping he would be lucky enough to hit the lion.

There was silence for a moment and then the lion roared. Patterson knew he had missed and fired again, but to no effect. He could only stand and listen to the lion eating one of his men.

The next morning the men refused to go to work. Instead they came to Patterson's tent. One of the foremen came forwards.

'Colonel Patterson,' he said. 'We have made a decision.'

'Yes,' said Patterson, 'what is it?'

'We are not staying here a day longer. We've heard that a witchdoctor has laid a curse on the railway line and set two devils to kill the men who work here.'

'They are not devils,' said Patterson, 'they are lions.'

'Devils or lions,' said the foreman, 'we came here to build a railway, not to be eaten alive. We are going home.'

He turned around and walked off. He was followed by a few dozen of the men, then a hundred more, then the whole mass of workmen set off. They picked up their bags and set off down the road that led to the coast.

Patterson was left standing alone. He stared after the workmen in shock and surprise. Suddenly anger boiled within him, a cold anger directed at the great cats who had been eating his men and had now caused the men to stop working on the railway. Patterson clenched his hands and stared wildly across the African plains; tucking a gun under his arm he set off with Mahini for the village of the Wa Jamousi.

'Good morning, Colonel Patterson,' said Engomani.

'Good morning, Engomani,' said Patterson, his anger turning to determination to destroy the lions. 'I need your help to kill the lions.'

Engomani nodded grimly, 'I shall do anything I can,' he said. 'The lions have killed thirty of my people. What do you need?'

'I need a donkey and people to help build a machan.'

'Of course you can have a donkey,' replied Engomani. 'But what is a machan?'

Patterson smiled; he had used an Indian word which Engomani could not understand. 'It is a wooden platform built on stilts where I can hide from the lion,' he explained.

Engomani nodded and organized a group of his tribesmen into a workteam. Patterson showed them how to build a machan four metres tall beside the deserted camp. As night fell Patterson climbed onto the machan. The men tied the donkey to a stake beside the machan, and sprinkled some blood on the ground to attract the lions.

For several hours Patterson waited alone on the machan. The moon came up, casting a pale light on the countryside, and moved slowly across the sky. Soon after midnight he heard a lion roar nearby, to be answered by a second lion. Then silence fell. The donkey became restless and brayed loudly. No sound came from the night.

Suddenly, a large lion burst from some bushes, sprang forwards and killed the donkey with a single bite on the neck. There had been no warning, no sound of the approaching lion and no movement in the bushes. Patterson was staggered by the speed of the attack and watched in shock for a moment, then he lifted his rifle, checked it was loaded and took careful aim.

Suddenly the whole machan rocked sideways, throwing Patterson from his feet. The platform swayed again and an angry roar split the silence. Patterson gripped hold of the platform and peered at the ground below. The second lion was staring up at him from the foot of the machan. It roared loudly again and threw itself at one of the machan supports, which gave way with a loud crack. If a second pole gave way Patterson would be thrown to the ground in front of the lions and killed instantly. Desperately grabbing his rifle, Patterson aimed at the lion and fired. The lion leapt sideways as the bullet plunged home, clawing at the air, before falling to the ground.

Patterson hurriedly reloaded his rifle and shot at the other lion. The lion jumped and snarled as the bullet struck, then it ran off into some bushes. Patterson heard the lion crashing through the undergrowth, then slowly the sounds died away as the lion fled. Patterson guessed it would not return to the donkey, so he curled up on the machan and fell asleep.

At dawn Patterson woke up to hear voices.

'Colonel Patterson,' called a voice, 'are you all right?'

Patterson looked over the edge of the machan

to see Mahini slowly approaching the body of the donkey.

'I'm up here,' called Patterson.

Mahini looked up and smiled broadly. 'I could not see you,' said Mahini. 'We heard the shooting. Did you kill the lions?'

'I killed one,' said Patterson as he climbed down from the machan. 'It's over here.'

Mahini came over with some other men. The dead lion was massive – over three metres in length. Patterson told the tribesmen to carry it back to their village.

'I wounded the other lion,' he told Mahini, 'so we shall have to follow it and kill it.'

Mahini nodded. 'If the lion is wounded it will not be far away.'

Patterson gave Mahini the shotgun. 'We shall go together. If we see the lion wait for me to fire first, the rifle is more accurate at a distance. But if it attacks us, shoot it with the shotgun.'

'Yes, sir,' said Mahini taking a firm grip on the gun.

Patterson found the track the lion had left as it ran away, leaving a trail of blood from its wounds. They carefully followed the tracks for over a mile until they led to a patch of dense bushes.

As Patterson and Mahini approached the bushes they heard a low growl. They peered cautiously into the bushes, but could not see the lion.

Suddenly it sprang out from under cover and came bounding forwards, snarling ferociously. Patterson raised his rifle and sent a bullet slamming into the beast's chest. The lion tumbled to the ground, then stood up and charged forwards again.

Patterson desperately tried to reload his rifle, but could not get the bullet into place.

'Shoot it!' he shouted at Mahini, but there was no reply.

Patterson glanced at Mahini. He was standing frozen with horror, his mouth hanging open and the gun useless in his hand. The lion was bounding forwards at great speed. In desperation Patterson threw down his gun and grabbed the shotgun from Mahini. He spun round to face the lion as it sprang forwards, jaws gaping and claws slashing through the air. Patterson did not have time to aim, but just lifted the gun and pulled the trigger. The shotgun crashed out, throwing Patterson backwards.

Patterson lay on the ground waiting to feel the claws of the lion. Instead there was only silence. He sat up. The lion lay dead just five metres in front of him, shot through the head.

Patterson went cold as he realized how close he had come to death. But he had won. The lions were dead, there would be no more killing and work could finally continue on the railway.

○ ○ ○

Eight years later, in 1900, another man-eating lion attacked a railway in East Africa. The lion ranged across the grasslands southeast of Nairobi in Kenya. It attacked those railway staff who worked at night.

On one occasion it tried to claw its way into a hut
built out of corrugated iron to reach the terrified
stationmaster inside.

On 5th June 1900 three police marksmen, named
Ryall, Hubner and Parenti set out to kill the lion.
After scouring the countryside for some days the
three hunters came to the small station of Kimaa.
The stationmaster at Kimaa said that the lion had
tried to attack one of his workmen the previous
night, but had been driven off by a burning torch.
He showed the three marksmen where this had happened and while they were searching the ground
Ryall found some tracks. Parenti and Hubner hurried to join their companion. In the damp sand they
saw the tracks of a large lion leading off to the west.

'He went off over there,' announced Parenti.
'Should we follow him?'

Ryall looked up at the sky. 'No,' he said. 'It will
be dark soon. We'll follow the tracks in the morning.' He turned to the stationmaster. 'Is there somewhere we can stay tonight?'

The stationmaster frowned. 'The hotel is full
tonight,' he said. 'But there is an old sleeping car
parked in a siding. You can sleep there.'

The four men walked back to the station. Parenti
thought that he heard something following them, but
he could not see anything. As night fell the three
hunters changed into their pyjamas and climbed into
the bunks on the railway sleeping car.

Some hours later Parenti was awoken by the slight
sound of a door swinging open. He opened his eyes
to see that the sliding door to the carriage was open.

Silhouetted against the bright moonlight beyond was a huge lion. It was standing still, gazing into the carriage. Parenti froze with terror. The men were supposed to be hunting the lion, not the other way around.

Parenti watched in horror as the lion stepped silently into the carriage. It trod on Parenti, who was almost beside himself with fear, and began sniffing at the bunks; moving forwards it shifted its great weight on to Parenti. The terrified man found he could hardly breathe with the weight of the lion on his chest.

Suddenly the lion lunged sideways, biting deep into Ryall. The doomed man screamed once, but was killed by a second bite. The scream awoke Hubner who looked down to see the lion biting into Ryall. Barely aware of what was happening Hubner leapt from his bunk. Flying over the back of the lion, he tumbled through the door and ran screaming towards the hotel.

Parenti, still pinned to the floor, saw the lion turn in alarm at the noise. Unable to breathe he watched as the beast grabbed Ryall's body in its teeth and leapt through a window, smashing the glass as it ran away.

Suddenly free of the lion, Parenti leapt to his feet and ran from the carriage; he tripped as he fled, tumbling to the ground. Springing to his feet Parenti ran on and collided with Hubner, followed by a group of armed guests and railway staff, coming the other way.

The men quickly lit torches and spread out, each

torchbearer accompanied by a gunman. They found Ryall's body a few metres from the carriage. Hubner thought he heard the lion moving through the bush a short distance away, but he was not certain. Carrying Ryall's body to the hotel, the men retreated to safety and locked the doors and windows, waiting for the dawn to come.

The following morning a new team of hunters arrived at Kimaa. They followed the tracks left by the lion, found it asleep beside a bush and shot it.

THE LUMBERING KILLERS

Bears are the largest and most powerful meat-eating animals on earth. Though classed as carnivores, bears will actually eat almost anything. They devour large quantities of berries in the autumn and will eat grass on occasion. But they remain very powerful hunters, whose paws are equipped with extremely long claws which can disable most other animals, including man, with a single blow.

There are several different types of bear, which live throughout Europe, Asia and America, but they are all bulky, muscular animals which walk on all fours. At one time bears were found in nearly every forested area on these continents, including Britain and New England. In most areas, however, the felling of the dense forests has meant that bears can no longer find enough food to survive and have become extinct. The commonest bear today is the brown bear, a two-metre long beast which lives throughout much of Asia and North America. It is the brown bear which has proved the most dangerous to man.

In the summer of 1908 a dozen Russian soldiers, led by Captain Golownin and Lieutenant Chlebnikoff escaped from a Japanese prisoner-of-war camp. The camp was on one of the heavily forested Kurile Islands off the east coast of Siberia, which then belonged to Japan. In order to escape from the island, the Russians had to march for many days through dense forest to a sheltered bay where Russian ships often stopped to collect water.

While making their break, the Russians had taken a sword, a pike and a shovel from the Japanese. They had also made off with a small quantity of food to sustain them on their long march through totally wild and unexplored forest. On their third night, the men were camping by a stream when one of the men heard a noise.

'What was that?' he said, looking up from placing a log on the fire.

The others listened. A long, low howl echoed through the forest.

'It's a wolf,' said Golownin.

'Wolves don't hunt alone,' observed one of the men. 'There'll be a whole pack of them on the move.'

'What should we do?' asked Chlebnikoff. 'They might attack us in the dark.'

Golownin looked around. 'There are plenty of twigs lying around,' he said. 'Let's make some torches so that we can use them to drive the wolves away. All wild animals are frightened of fire.'

The men agreed that this was a good idea, and began collecting twigs from the forest floor. One man approached a patch of bushes, where many small sticks lay on the ground. Suddenly he leapt backwards with a cry of alarm.

'What is it?' asked Golownin.

'There's something in there,' said the man. 'I heard it growl.'

Golownin came up to the man and stared at the bushes. There was no sign of anything in them.

'There doesn't seem to be anything there,' said Golownin, 'but we'd better stay clear just in case.'

Even as he spoke there was a ferocious snarl followed by the sound of crashing branches. Charging out of the bushes at top speed came a huge bear, snarling with anger and baring its sharp teeth. The men scattered in fright to hide behind trees, but Golownin drew his sword and stood firm.

As the lumbering bear came up to him, Golownin dodged sideways and brought the sword slamming down. The blade struck the back of the bear's skull, and instantly snapped in two.

The maddened bear swung round and growled angrily at Golownin. The officer stood with the shattered stump of the sword in his hand, staring in horror at his attacker. With a grunt the bear launched itself forwards, threatening to claw Golownin to the ground.

At the last moment Chlebnikoff snatched up the spade and sprang forwards. He brought the flat of the spade down hard on the bear's nose, causing it to rear upwards in pain. One of the men, taking his lead from the officers, grabbed the pike which had been leaning against a tree. He ran forwards, driving the weapon deep into the bear's chest. The beast pawed the air once, then toppled over, dead.

The men gazed at the dead bear, realizing how close they had come to death. For a moment nobody moved. Then a wolf howled and the men scattered to collect more twigs. The pack, however, did not come near them during the night. Next day they continued their march and after two days reached the coast where they were later rescued.

○ ○ ○

Two large types of bear live in North America, the black bear and the grizzly bear. The black bear is very like the brown bear which attacked Golownin in both size and behaviour. But the grizzly is much larger, being nearly three metres long and weighing over 700 kilogrammes.

In the autumn of 1963 the black bears of Canada and Alaska became very dangerous and some took to maneating. The reason for this was a food shortage. Because of the poor summer weather, bushes in the area had not produced many berries. The bears became extremely hungry and were likely to attack anything which looked like food.

One man unfortunate enough to be thought of as food by a black bear was Charles Major. Major and a friend, named Henderson, were on a hunting trip, looking for moose and deer to stock their larders. As night fell on the third day of their trip Major and Henderson pitched camp.

They erected their little tent and cooked a meal of bacon and vegetables over a small fire. As the moon rose, Major climbed into the tent, tucking himself up in his sleeping bag. Henderson sat up for some time, reading by the light of a gas lamp. Finishing a chapter of his book, Henderson stretched and then climbed into his own sleeping bag. Before long he drifted off into deep slumber.

Soon afterwards a large black bear came shambling past the camp. It had been searching for food all day long, but had found little to satisfy its hunger. Only a few berries could be found, and the bear was ravenous.

The bear caught the scent of bacon and felt its hunger even more. The smell was appetizing and promised to end the gnawing ache which had troubled the bear for so long. It waddled towards the source of the smell.

It found a small pile of glowing wood embers. The bear was frightened of fire, but this one seemed to be going out. By the light of the pale moon the bear could make out a pile of strangely shaped objects, some of which smelt delicious.

The bear nosed among the plates and frying pan. They had not been washed properly and the smell of food was strong. The bear licked the plates, savouring the taste of food, but there was no food to satisfy the hunger which was growing with every passing moment.

Then the bear caught a strange and unfamiliar scent coming from the odd shaped object beyond the fire. Cautiously the bear moved towards the tent and stuck its head inside.

The bear did not recognize the smell of man, but it could make out two animals lying in the tent. The animals were rather larger than the bear would normally attack for it preferred to prey on animals which it could kill without danger to itself. However the animals appeared to be asleep and the hunger within the bear decided it on taking a risk.

With a sudden lunge the bear sank its jaws deep into the nearest figure. At once there was a loud scream. The bear pulled back, dragging the creature from the tent. The shouting continued, but this did not worry the bear, the animals it attacked often screamed and roared before they died.

The bear saw the second animal standing up, but it was staying back. The bear thought it could not be hurt so long as the other animal could not reach it with any claws or teeth. The bear let go of its prey and snarled at the second animal. That should warn it to stay away.

Gripping the first animal in its mouth once more the bear began dragging it away towards some bushes. It was still shouting loudly so the bear struck it with its claws, but the screaming continued. The bear knew it could kill the animal once it was in the shelter of the bushes.

The bear noticed the second animal behaving strangely. Instead of either running away or trying to attack the bear it was standing still. The bear saw the animal lift a strange, long object to its shoulder and point it at the bear.

There was a loud bang.

The bear felt a savage pain strike through its shoulder. It roared in agony, looking round for the animal which had attacked it.

The bang sounded again, and again the pain came. The bear felt strength draining from its muscles. It slid to the ground and lay still.

Henderson put his rifle down. He had pumped two large calibre bullets into the bear. Suddenly uncertain, he lifted his rifle and reloaded it before picking up a stone. He threw it at the motionless bear, striking it on the head. It did not move. The bear was dead.

Realizing this, Henderson raced forwards.

'Are you badly hurt?' he asked Major.

Major groaned out loud. 'My leg hurts,' he said.

Henderson moved round to look at his friends leg. It had been badly cut and chewed by the bear.

'Hang on,' he said, 'I'll get the medical chest.'

Henderson ran back to the tent and scrabbled around inside. He soon found the box of medicines and hurried back to his friend.

Quickly tearing off Major's trouser leg, Henderson doused the wound with antiseptic. Major gasped in pain as the antiseptic took effect. Working quickly to stop the bleeding, Henderson wrapped tight bandages around his friend's leg before carrying him back to the tent and giving him some pain-killing drugs.

Next morning Henderson carried Major back to their automobile and drove him to a hospital. The doctor hurried Major into the operating room where he sewed the wounds and dressed them properly. Major was soon out of hospital and within a few weeks was able to walk again. He was a lucky man to survive such a vicious attack.

○ ○ ○

Michele Koons was very unlucky. She happened to be in the wrong place at the wrong time and paid with her life. In August 1967 Michele and four friends, Ron and Ray Noseck, Paul Dunn and Denise Huckle went camping in Glacier National Park. Unlike the others Paul Dunn had never been camping before, so when his friends suggested that they should go to Glacier National Park in the Rockies, Paul jumped at the chance.

They set out on a long hike which involved camping out at night. The five youngsters carried tents and cooking equipment with them. As the afternoon sun began to set they found themselves beside a lake, where forests swept down on to the shore line. Finding a patch of open ground beside the lake, they decided to pitch camp.

The three young men went fishing, returning with several fine catches. Within minutes a fire had been built and the fish were grilling ready for supper.

Michele happened to glance up, and squeaked in alarm.

'There's a . . . a bear!' she shouted in alarm.

The others looked up to see a huge grizzly bear wandering lazily out of the trees heading directly for their camp. Barely stopping to think, Paul sprang to his feet and ran in the opposite direction. Glancing over his shoulder he saw the others following him.

When he had covered some fifty metres, Paul

campsite, collected the sleeping bags and retreated to the new site.

They started a large fire, and arranged the sleeping bags around it. The new camp was out of sight of the old one, and the five youngsters felt fairly safe. They had been told before entering the park that bears only bothered people if the people bothered them and the youngsters were determined to stay by their fire and avoid bears.

Soon they fell asleep.

Some hours later Paul woke up, but could not think what had awakened him. Then he heard a loud splash made by some animal down by the lakeshore. He looked at his luminous watch to find that it was 4.30 in the morning, two hours before dawn.

He sat up and looked around. The fire had died down and almost gone out. He reached to throw some wood on the glowing embers when the splash came again. He looked towards the lake, but at first could see nothing. Then he saw something move, a vague shadow in the night. Seconds later he got the shock of his life.

Lumbering into the light thrown by the dying fire was a massive grizzly bear. Its fur was wet and dripping and its mouth hung open, revealing long sharp fangs. Overcome with fright, Paul pulled the flap of his sleeping bag over his head and lay still. Perhaps the bear would go away.

In the darkness, Paul could hear the sounds of sniffing. The bear was nosing around the campsite, probably looking for more food. The sniffing became louder as the bear came closer. Paul lay still in terror, quaking at the sound of the bear sniffing around his sleeping bag.

Paul felt a heavy pressure on his sleeping bag as the bear placed its feet on him. He had trouble breathing and almost whimpered with fright. Then the pressure was gone, but the bear was sniffing around his head. The sniffing stopped and for a long, terrible moment there was absolute silence.

Then the bear bit, sinking its teeth deep into the sleeping bag, but only slightly scratching Paul. Forced into action by sheer, uncontrollable terror, Paul sprang from his bag, crashing heavily into the bear as he did so. The bear reared on his hind legs, claws slashing through the air. Ducking sideways, Paul ran screaming towards a tree. He leapt at the branches and pulled himself up. Scrambling and scrabbling upwards, Paul scaled ten metres before he dared stop climbing.

Gasping for breath, Paul stared down to see the bear standing under the tree, gazing up at him. Paul breathed heavily to catch his breath and looked towards the fire. Ron and Denise were sitting up and looking round to see what had happened.

'Run,' shouted Paul. 'The bear tried to kill me.'

Ron leapt to his feet, seeming to see the bear for the first time, and dragged Denise from her sleeping bag.

'Come on,' he shouted running towards a tall tree. He stopped briefly to kick his brother awake. 'Get up,' he said. 'The bear has come back.' Then he raced after Denise. He reached the tree seconds after the girl and followed her up into the branches.

Paul watched Ron and Denise escape, but saw Ray and Michele were still in danger.

'Ray,' he shouted desperately. 'The bear, the bear.'

Ray was awake now, and gazing around him. Paul watched as the bear left his tree and walked back to the fire. As he saw the bear, Ray sprang to his feet. He stooped to shake Michele awake, but the bear was almost upon him. Taking to his heels, Ray ran off as fast as he could, reaching the tree next to Ron and Denise.

The bear stooped and began sniffing at Michele's sleeping bag. Suddenly the bear grunted and slammed his jaws into the sleeping bag. Michele screamed. The bear clawed the bag, ripping it to shreds, and bit again. The screaming stopped at once. Michele was dead.

The bear gripped the dead girl firmly and dragged the body away from the fire into the forest. Paul watched the scene in horror. He had no idea that wild animals could be so dangerous. Nobody had warned him and he was unprepared for horror on such a scale.

'What happened?' shouted Ray.

Paul was too shocked to answer.

'Paul,' called Ray again. 'We can't see from here. What has happened?'

'The bear has got Michele,' shouted Paul. 'It just killed her and took her away.'

There was a stunned silence from the others. Paul began to cry, feeling alone and vulnerable sitting in his tree. He wiped his eyes on his arm.

'Right,' called Ron's voice from the darkness. 'Now listen to me. We've got to stay calm.' Even as he spoke Ron's voice cracked, revealing the fear he felt. 'We can't do anything because we haven't got guns. Everyone stay in your trees until the morning. Then we shall go for help.'

Paul knew Ron was talking sense, but the dark forest seemed to be pushing in. He was certain he could see the shadows of bears moving in the darkness, waiting to pounce on him as one had on Michele. He shuddered and gripped the tree tighter, waiting for the pale sky of dawn.

When the sun eventually came up, Paul climbed down from his tree and joined the others. He felt stiff and cold from his uncomfortable night, and was still frightened that the bear would return to the attack.

'We'd better get to the Ranger Station,' said Paul.

'Yes,' said Ron, 'let's go.'

It took two hours to trek to the Station. When they got there they told Ranger Landa all about their night of terror. Landa turned pale – he had never heard of a bear attacking a human before and was unsure what to do about it.

Hurriedly, he radioed the Park Headquarters for instructions. They told him that help was on the way, but instructed him to try to shoot the bear before it got away.

Picking up his rifle and plenty of ammunition, Landa set off towards the lake. He took Paul with him as a guide, and left the others at the Station.

It was late in the day by the time Landa and

Paul reached the devastated campsite. They began searching the surrounding area and soon found Michele's partly eaten body in the forest. Soon afterwards a ranger named Gildert arrived. He was an expert marksman and had been sent by Headquarters to help Landa shoot the bear. By this time darkness was closing in again, so the men trekked to a small cabin two miles away for the night.

Early next morning Gildert emerged from the cabin into the pale sunlight of dawn. Almost at once he saw a bear watching him from the forest. It was big and pale, just like the bear which had killed Michele.

'Landa,' called Gildert softly, 'fetch the guns and load them. The bear is here.'

At the sound of the human voice, the bear ducked from sight, hiding in the bushes. Landa emerged from the hut and gave Gildert his rifle, holding his own firmly. He looked around in silence, but could see nothing.

'Where is it?' he asked.

'In those bushes,' replied Gildert. 'It hid when I spoke.'

For several long seconds the men scanned the bushes in silence, but nothing happened.

'Perhaps it has gone,' whispered Landa.

Gildert shook his head. He was certain he would have heard the bear if it had moved far.

Suddenly the bear crashed into sight, tearing across the strip of open ground towards the two men. Grunting savagely the bear came on at full speed, its muscles rippling as it ran.

Gildert lifted his rifle and took careful aim. His finger closed around the trigger and his gun roared. A split second later Landa's gun blazed and the bear fell dead.

As the sound of the gunshots died away, the men remained still and silent. Landa slowly lowered his gun to the ground.

'It was trying to kill us,' he said softly.

Gildert nodded slowly. 'I've never known a bear do that before,' he muttered in surprise. 'I've known bears attack when they were disturbed, but that bear was trying to hunt us for food. It was a real maneater.'

THE SILENT KILLERS

Sharks are very possibly the most feared man-eating animals of all. Recent films and books about sharks have boosted their reputation for ferocity and man-killing. While it is a fact that many people have been killed by sharks, the danger is not as great as imagined. Far more people die each year from snake-bites, for instance!

Yet there is something particularly horrible about death in a shark's jaws. The shark is a graceful animal which swims constantly through the oceans with only one apparent motive, to kill and eat as many other animals as possible. Perhaps it is this single-minded determination which gives the shark its aura of terror.

The shark is superbly adapted to killing. Its jaws are equipped with savagely sharp teeth, able to tear their way through living flesh, and their stomachs can hold vast amounts of fresh meat. The shark's senses are finely tuned to finding prey. They can detect blood at distances of many kilometres and are able to track it down to its source. Many fishermen have been amazed at how quickly sharks gather when bait is dropped into the sea.

There are many hundreds of different types of shark, most of which are quite small and are no danger to man. But some species are much larger and are capable of killing a man in seconds. Perhaps the most famous is the great white, a rather rare creature, which can grow to over eight metres in length and can swallow a man whole. Other large sharks include the blue, hammerhead and whaler sharks, all of which have attacked humans and which swim in the warmer oceans of the world in large numbers.

Gianluco Costanzo helped his father, Luciano, strap the air tanks to his back. Luciano was a highly experienced skindiver and underwater photographer. On 4th February 1989, he was on a spear-fishing trip with his son and a friend named Paolo Bader.

They had left the Italian fishing village of Piombino early in the morning in their nine-metre motor boat. Now, with the sun climbing high into the sky, Luciano was preparing for his first dive. Gianluco adjusted his father's weighted belt and grinned at him as he handed over the spear gun.

'Try to catch something good for supper,' he said.

'Don't worry,' said Luciano Costanzo to his son. 'I should get something tasty.'

It was a normal day's spear-fishing for the Constanzo men and their friend. They had no reason to think that tragedy was just moments away.

Luciano slipped backwards into the clear waters of the Mediterranean. Gianluco watched his father for a few seconds as he slid away towards the seabed, twenty-five metres beneath the boat. Then he turned back to the deck of the boat. His own equipment needed sorting out before he could join his father in the water.

'I hope we catch plenty today,' said Gianluco.

'I wouldn't have thought we would have too much trouble,' replied Paolo. 'The tide is just turning, and that's a good time to find fish in the bay.'

Gianluco nodded. He had been fishing with his father for over ten years now, ever since the first trip on his ninth birthday. Only a few times had they returned to Piombino without enough fish for a meal. Usually they had more than enough and passed the spares around their friends. The sport of spear-fishing was both exciting and rewarding.

Suddenly there was a loud shout. Gianluco spun round to see his father about twenty metres away, swimming desperately towards the boat.

'Help, help,' shouted Luciano.

Gianluco dashed to the side of the boat, getting ready to help his father into the boat.

'What is it, Dad?' he called. 'What's wrong?'

'It's a shark,' screamed Luciano.

'Look!' exclaimed Paolo. 'Behind him.'

Gianluco scanned the sea behind his father. Cutting through the surface like a knife was a thin upright fin. Light grey in colour, the fin stood several centimetres clear of the water and was broad triangular in shape.

Leaping to the rear of the boat, Gianluco tried to start the engine. He hoped to move towards his father or perhaps he could frighten the shark away. The motor did not start first time. Gianluco glanced towards his father, now just fifteen metres away. As Gianluco watched the shark's fin circled around

stopped. The others came up to join him. Paul pointed back towards the camp.

'There goes our supper,' he said.

The bear was eating the fish and other food in the camp. It grunted in satisfaction and licked its lips as it ate. Once it looked towards the group of frightened youngsters, but otherwise took no notice of them. After about fifteen minutes, the bear had finished its meal and lumbered away into the woods.

'What should we do?' asked Paul. He did not know how to react to wild animals.

'I think we should head for the Ranger Station,' said Michele.

'Don't be ridiculous,' said Ray. 'The Station is in the same direction as the bear has gone. We might meet it in the forest.'

'What about the camping ground?' suggested Denise.

'No' said Ray. 'The ground is over three miles away and it is nearly dark. It would be pitch black before we got there. I think we should stay here.'

'What about the bear?' asked Ron anxiously. 'It might come back looking for more food.'

'True,' said Ray. 'I know. We'll make a new camp a little distance away and build a large fire. If the bear comes back it'll go to the old campsite and the fire should keep it away from our new site.'

The others agreed that this was a good idea. They gathered plenty of firewood and found a new campsite on some open ground uphill from the old site. Ray and Ron cautiously approached the old

Luciano twice, each time drawing closer. Then it dived from sight.

Gianluco abandoned the engine and stepped to the side of the boat. He reached out his arms towards his father, now barely ten metres away. A few seconds longer and he would be able to pull him from the now dangerous ocean.

With a sudden scream of pain, Luciano surged up from the water. Spray fountained around him as he rose, drops of seawater catching the noon sun and sparkling like jewels. Gianluco stared in amazement. Then his amazement turned to horror.

Thrusting his father from the water, and gripping him around the waist, was a gigantic shark. So large was the beast that it had its mouth completely around Luciano with his legs in its throat. Gianluco screamed in terror as the large fish plunged back into the water, carrying Luciano with it. The shark vanished beneath the sea in a boiling mass of swirling water.

As Paolo and Gianluco watched, the water where Luciano had been slowly turned red with blood. Without a word the two men stared at the sea for a long time. Suddenly breaking himself free from the shock, Gianluco ran back to the engine, got it started and drove the boat towards the fatal spot.

The triangular fin of the shark cut the surface of the sea some distance away. Gianluco steered the boat round in a graceful curve and gave chase. The fish dived from sight. Though Gianluco and Paolo searched the area for some time they did not see the shark again. All they found of Luciano were a few pieces of his wetsuit.

○ ○ ○

The attack on Luciano Constanza caused a sensation. Such attacks are rare off the Italian coast, and the authorities sprang into action. Local fishermen were hired to try to catch the killer fish, thought to be a great white shark. Experts were flown in to predict where the shark might have gone and how best to trap it, but to no avail. The shark was never caught. Slowly the fuss died down and Piombino became a sleepy fishing village once again.

○ ○ ○

Most shark attacks are launched on lone swimmers in the ocean, like the attack on Luciano, though the time of day and depth of water seems to be of no importance to the shark. If it is hungry and comes across a human it will attack. A classic example of this occurred in Puerto Rico in around 1860.

The sailing ship *Kipling* entered a Puerto Rico harbour on the afternoon tide and anchored a short distance from shore. Boats came out to her to take off the cargo of cotton cloth which was due to be dropped off there. When the last bale of cloth had been swung over the side and into the waiting boat, the sailors went below to rest.

Joe lay in his bunk, staring at the ceiling of the cabin. He had worked hard all day and felt like snatching a short doze. A finger prodded into his ribs, disturbing his rest.

'Here Joe,' said Adam. 'Will you be coming ashore with the rest of us for a drink and some fun?'

'I'd love to,' said Joe, 'but the mate has me on extra duties if you remember.'

'That mate,' scowled Adam. 'He's got no right to punish us the way he does. The slightest thing wrong and he comes down on us like a ton of bricks.'

'Too true,' replied Joe. 'All I did was polish the brass rail on the quarterdeck too slowly, and here I am with extra duties for a week.'

'Listen, Joe,' said Adam, glancing around to make sure nobody was listening. 'Why don't you skip ship tonight?'

'What do you mean?' asked Joe.

'Well,' continued Adam, 'the mate likes an evening drink and once it gets past ten he's usually fast asleep. If we all go ashore at seven like we intended, you wait till the mate nods off and then slip over the side and swim ashore to join us.'

'I don't know,' said Joe. 'If I get caught, it'll just mean more punishment for me.'

'Tell you what,' said George. 'We'll be waiting on the dockside around half past ten. If you get the chance then come to join us, if not we'll wait awhile then go to a pub.'

'OK,' agreed Joe. 'We'll see what happens.'

Later that evening the sailors went ashore as arranged, while Joe stayed on board scrubbing the deck clean. He smiled as his companions passed and winked at them. If he could possibly slip away, Joe was determined to do so.

Soon after ten, however, Joe heard the sound of snoring coming from the mate's cabin. He crept quietly to the door and peeked in to see the mate slumped over his desk fast asleep. Carefully packing away the scrubbing brush and bucket, Joe made ready to swim ashore.

After tying his shoes around his neck and wrapping his money in a leather pouch around his waist, Joe took a deep breath and dived into the warm water. Swimming steadily Joe struck out for the dockside where his friends would be waiting.

Suddenly a loud shout from behind him made Joe turn around. The mate was standing on the deck of the ship yelling at him. As Joe watched the man lifted a gun to his shoulder and fired.

Joe was suddenly frightened and thought that the mate must have gone mad, shooting at a man for slipping off for the evening. Joe ploughed forwards through the water as fast as he could. A loud splash told him that the mate had followed him into the water. Desperately Joe swam for the shore, hoping to reach his friends before the mate caught up with him.

Suddenly Joe heard a terrible scream – a cry of great terror and pain. Turning around in panic Joe could see nothing but the moonlit water and the ship resting at anchor. The mate had disappeared!

Suddenly frightened, Joe swam for the shore. As

he approached the stone jetty he saw several figures standing waiting.

'Come on, Joe,' shouted one. 'Hurry!'

Joe recognized Adam's voice and headed for the man. As he reached the stone wall, eager hands reached down and grasped his arms, pulling him bodily out of the water.

'Are you all right, Joe?' asked George.

Joe nodded.

'What happened?' he gasped.

'When the mate jumped and followed you,' Adam told him, 'he didn't get very far. Soon after he hit the surface of the water we saw a shark fin cutting through the moonlit water close behind him. The fin swam around behind the mate, than ran up close to him. The mate screamed, lifted his arms in the air and then vanished. The shark must have dragged him under.'

Joe shuddered despite the warm weather.

'You mean the mate's been eaten by a shark?' he asked.

'Looks that way,' said Adam.

'And it nearly got me,' gasped Joe.

'True,' said George. 'but look on the bright side.'

Joe stared at his friend in surprise. 'What bright side?' he asked.

'Well,' said George, 'the mate won't be giving us any unfair punishments any more. Who said sharks bring bad luck to a ship?'

Helping Joe to his feet, the men made their way to tavern where Joe was able to dry out. Next morning they returned to the ship to find the captain looking for the mate. The sailors knew what had happened, but they did not want Joe to get into any trouble for his part in the tragedy, so they said nothing.

The captain waited in Puerto Rico for three days, waiting for the mate to return to the ship. But the *Kipling* had a cargo to deliver to St Kitts and the captain could afford to wait no longer. Thinking that the mate might have joined another ship which offered higher pay, or that he was lying drunk somewhere, the captain left Puerto Rico.

○ ○ ○

Such attacks on lone swimmers are by far the commonest type of shark attack, although only a handful of swimmers are killed each year throughout the world. But they are not the most frightening and horrific forms of shark attack. The worst attacks occur when a mob of sharks rampage in a frenzied search for food.

Sometimes sharks swim together in large groups of several hundred. If such a mob finds a large source of food, such as a shoal of herring, they go into a frenzy, biting anything which moves. When such an attack is directed at humans it is a truly awful event.

One such attack occurred in 1942 during World War Two as the Canadian troopship *Nova Scotia* was carrying 762 Italian prisoners of war and their guards to Cape Town where they were to be imprisoned. Sergeant Piet van der Post checked his rifle was loaded and then cocked it. He nodded to his friend, Sergeant Clark Jones, who then opened the door to the room where some of the Italian prisoners were kept. Piet watched the South African soldiers carry in the trays of food and kept his rifle aimed at the Italians. The prisoners had caused no trouble on the long voyage south, but there was no sense in taking any chances.

The trays of food were put on the tables and the prisoners took their places. As the guards made their way back to the door, Piet relaxed and lowered his rifle. Suddenly a massive blast ripped through the ship, throwing Piet to the ground. The sound of the explosion had scarcely died away when smoke billowed into the room. Piet sat up and shook his head. He wondered what had happened. Something was wrong, that much was clear.

Quickly scrambling to his feet, Piet shouted at the Italians to leave the room. He could not leave them to choke in a room filled with smoke. The deck beneath Piet's feet lurched to one side, resting at an awkward angle. A claxon alarm began to sound, filling the ship with its strident blasts. The Italians poured out of the room to gather on the deck outside.

The PA system crackled into life.

'This is the captain speaking,' said the voice on the PA. 'We have been struck by a torpedo. Abandon ship. I repeat. Abandon ship.'

'We must be sinking,' Piet shouted to Clark. The deck shifted again as if to add urgency to his words.

'We must get these men into lifejackets and launch

the boats,' said Clark. He turned to the group of prisoners. 'Come on,' he shouted. 'Follow me.' He waved his arms to get the message across to the Italians and ran towards the room where the lifejackets were kept. Ripping open the door, Clark and Piet hurriedly distributed the jackets and then led the men towards the rear of the ship where the boats were kept.

An explosion shook the ship from end to end and a huge column of smoke and flame shot up from a great gash in the hull. The ship shuddered and dropped deeper into the water, causing the green seawater to surge over the rail and run across the decks.

'There's no time for the boats,' shouted Piet. 'Over the side and swim for it.' He vaulted over the rail into the open ocean. The water was quite warm and his lifejacket kept him afloat. Knowing that the turbulence set up by the sinking ship would drag him under, Piet swam away from the ship as fast as he could.

Having covered over a hundred metres, Piet stopped swimming and turned around. Some of the boats had been launched, but most were still on the ship. Hundreds of men were bobbing around in the sea. He gazed back at the ship, now awash with water. Another explosion boomed out and the funnel crashed forwards onto the decks. Suddenly the ship slid forwards and down, disappearing beneath the surface.

One of the boats rowed slowly through the crowd of men floating on the sea. On board was a man in a naval uniform. Piet recognized him as the First Mate of the ship.

'Come on,' said Piet to Clark who was a few metres away, 'let's see what the officer has to say.'

Together the two men swam over to the boat. Many other men had had the same idea and were gathering around the lifeboat. The other men in lifejackets were gathering round other lifeboats.

'Now listen to me,' shouted the officer. 'We are a hundred miles off the South African coast. Normally I would order the lifeboats to row that distance, it might take a day or two. But I can't leave you all in the water.'

'Thank goodness for that,' commented Clark.

'So,' continued the officer, 'we shall stay here with you. I have decided to send one boat to the coast to fetch help. The captain went down with the ship so I do not know if he managed to send off a radio message before the ship sank. If he did we should receive help within a few hours. If not we shall have to wait for the boat to reach shore.'

'I hope the captain got a message out,' said Piet. 'I don't fancy bobbing around like this for a couple of days.'

The officer was speaking again. 'Until such time as we are rescued I want you all to keep together. We shall lash the boats together with rope and pass ropes around for all you men in the water to hang on to. If we stay together we stand a better chance of being seen and rescued. Also I want the badly wounded men in the boat, they'll stand a better chance in the dry.'

Soon ropes were being passed around the men in the water and between the lifeboats. One boat set off towards the coast.

'I hope they hurry up and get to land,' said Piet.

'So do I,' said Clark. 'This is not very entertaining.'

The end of the rope reached Piet so he grabbed hold and tied it around his waist before passing it on to Clark, who then passed it to the men beyond him. Soon all the men were holding onto the ropes and were firmly linked together. Some hours passed without anything happening. Once or twice Piet thought he had heard an aircraft engine, but nothing had come into sight.

'Sir,' shouted a voice suddenly. It came from one of the men floating behind Piet. The officer stood up in the boat. 'Yes,' he called.

'This man's dead, sir,' said the voice.

'All right,' said the officer. 'Stay calm. Untie him from the ropes and set him adrift. There's nothing we can do for him now.'

'Right, sir,' called the voice. Soon Piet saw the body floating away from the group.

About an hour later a second man died and was set adrift. Soon the wounded men were dying rapidly. Within a further hour ten men had died.

'Sir,' called a voice from the fringes of the group. There was a definite note of worry in the voice.

The officer stood up again. 'Yes,' he called.

'There's a *shark*, sir.'

The officer strained his eyes to see beyond the

group. Piet tried to follow his eyes, but could not see beyond the heads of the men in front of him.

A scream suddenly rang out, followed by a shout.

'The shark's got him,' shouted a panic-striken voice. 'The shark's got him.'

There was a sudden move as the men near the shark tried to move away, pushing against those beside them. A man swam into Piet, who had to move aside.

'Calm down,' shouted the officer. 'You'll only excite the thing. I think it's gone away,' he added.

For several minutes nothing further happened. The sun continued to beat down on the sea. Piet was thirsty and he wondered if the lifeboats had any water on board. But then thoughts of water were driven from his mind.

'Sharks,' shouted someone. 'Lots of them.'

'Keep calm,' shouted the officer. 'They might go away if we all stay still.'

'I'll bet those devils have smelt the blood of the wounded men,' said Clark, 'that's what's brought them here.'

The men started screaming as the sharks pulled them under the water. Soon the sharks were swirling around the whole group, slashing the men with their teeth.

Piet noticed in shock that the seawater was turning red with blood. The sound of screaming and shouting was becoming deafening. Some men tried to climb onto one of the boats. They scrambled at the sides of the boat in their efforts to get aboard. With a sudden flip the boat turned upside down, throwing the wounded men into the sea to be devoured by the sharks.

Piet felt something brush against his leg. Then it was gone. He saw Clark jerk convulsively, then lie still.

'Are you all right?' asked Piet.

His friend did not answer, so Piet shook his friend by the shoulder. As Clark slowly turned over Piet saw that he had been bitten in half by a shark. Only his chest, arms and head remained. Piet yelled in terror and then fainted.

He came to some time later to find himself almost alone. Two of the boats had vanished, as had most of the men in the water. Piet swam to the side of a boat. Several hours later a ship arrived at the scene of the sinking and rescued the survivors. There were nearly a thousand men on board the *Nova Scotia* when she had sunk – only two hundred survived the sinking and the terrible attacks of the sharks.

o o o

Sharks are not the only dangerous fish in the world. The terror they inspire is equalled by a small fish, scarcely twenty centimetres long, which lives in the rivers and lakes of South America. This is the piranha, a freshwater fish which feeds on other fish and on any land animal which falls into the water. The black piranha, the most dangerous species, has needle-sharp teeth which can nip a piece of flesh from a victim with the neatness of a razor blade.

It is not the teeth alone which make the piranha such a deadly animal. There is its habit of swimming in vast shoals, several hundred strong, and of cruising along rivers in search of prey. When a victim appears, the shoal attacks, ripping the victim apart in seconds. The people who live beside the waterways of South America are terrified of the fish, particularly as it is not always possible to tell when piranhas are close by.

Manuel Colonga was one man who witnessed the terrible power of the piranha. In 1934 Manuel was travelling up the Rio Jufari in Brazil. He was going upriver to visit a relative who owned a small rubber plantation at Demini in the midst of the rainforest.

Transport through the dense forest was next to impossible, so Manuel was going upriver in a large canoe paddled by locals. He shared the canoe with half-a-dozen other passengers, one of whom had a small pig.

Manuel sat in the canoe, watching the endless green forest slip by on either side. The pig refused to stay still, but continually moved around the floor of the canoe. When its owner tied a string around its neck and held it securely, it squealed loudly.

Manuel leapt forward and tapped the man with the pig on the shoulder.

'Excuse me,' he said. 'But do you mind if I ask why you are carrying a pig upriver?'

'Ah, Señor,' said the man. 'I am taking him to my cousin. My cousin keeps pigs, but his swine are small and puny. This pig,' the man patted the animal on the head, 'is the son of a fine, big pig. My cousin wants to add this animal to his herd so that he will have big pigs in the future.'

'Oh,' said Manuel. 'And where does your cousin live?'

'He is the chief cook on a rubber plantation at Demini and he needs the pigs to use in the kitchens.'

Manuel smiled. 'My uncle runs a plantation at Demini,' he said. 'Perhaps I shall eat some of your cousin's pigs while I am there.'

'Perhaps,' said the man. 'My cousin is a very fine cook. If you are lucky he will invite you for a meal.'

At that moment the pig squirmed free of the man's grasp and leapt over the side of the canoe. It struck out as if swimming for the river bank two dozen metres away.

'Excuse me, Señor,' said the man to Manuel. He began pulling on his piece of string, dragging the pig back towards the boat.

Suddenly the water around the pig erupted as if a wind had whipped up some waves. The pig squealed loudly then fell silent and slipped beneath the water. The surface continued to churn into wavelets and swirls. The water began to turn red.

'Piranha!' shouted a woman next to Manuel. The man stopped pulling in his pig. After a few seconds the disturbance ceased and died away. The man pulled in his string, but all that was attached to the far end were a few bones, stripped clean of flesh. The pig had gone, devoured in seconds by the piranha.

The man stared at the bones in disappointment and then flung them into the river.

'Piranha,' he spat. 'They are devils. They eat my

pig. Ten years ago, they ate my cousin's wife's sister. They will eat anything in the river.'

Manuel could only stare at the river in shock and fear. He made a promise to himself never to go swimming in the Rio Jufari.

HUNTING BY NUMBERS

Wolves are powerful hunters, related to domestic dogs, standing one metre tall and equipped with a fearsome array of sharp teeth. These weapons are highly effective, but the wolves owe their success to the fact that they hunt in groups. As many as two dozen wolves may live and hunt together in a pack.

The wolves are very cunning and co-operate with each other. Sometimes one wolf will cause a diversion while the others dash in for the kill. Normally wolves hunt deer and other wild animals, but when pressed by hunger they will attack man. As with most large carnivores, the wolves have been pushed out of many of their original homelands by man. Wolves frequently attacked farm animals such as cattle and sheep, so farmers killed wolves whenever they had the chance. Wolves once lived throughout Europe, Asia and America, but now they only survive in remote areas such as dense forests and high mountains.

In the 1820s wolves were still very common throughout most of Europe, and infested the vast forests of Russia in huge numbers. It was at this time that the Scotsman William Wilson had to travel through Russia to the city of St Petersburg, now called Leningrad. Wilson hired a coach and a driver named Maletov for the long journey through the dense forests. He loaded his luggage into the back of the coach and sat beside the coachman, or *yemstchik*.

For several days the two men travelled through the forests without anything unusual happening at all. They passed through several villages and one or two small towns, stopping at local inns for the night. The journey was comfortable and Wilson was enjoying visiting the local sights.

On the seventh morning of the journey, Maletov seemed slightly worried when they set out. He checked the horses and the harness twice before he would allow Wilson to climb into the coach.

'Is something wrong?' asked Wilson.

'I hope not,' replied the *yemstchik*. 'But the land-lord told me last night that the local wolves are very hungry.'

Wilson was rather puzzled. There were no wolves in Scotland and he did not know about the dangers presented by the animals.

'I don't understand,' he said. 'What has that got to do with us?'

Maletov shrugged. 'They might give us some trouble,' he said. 'I wanted to be certain that the horses were in good condition.'

With that he climbed up into the driving seat and cracked his whip. The horses set off at a brisk walk, pulling the coach along the muddy road into the forest.

A few hours after noon they reached a small

village where they stopped for a meal. As Wilson finished his meal Maletov came up to him.

'Excuse me, sir,' he said 'but I think we should stay here tonight.'

'Here?' asked Wilson in surprise. 'But it is nowhere near dark yet. We should travel on to the next village.'

'It is a long distance to the next inn,' said Maletov, 'and it might be dark before we get there.'

'We have travelled after dark before,' said Wilson. 'I mustn't be late reaching St Petersburg. I say we push on.'

The *yemstchik* looked disappointed. 'As you say, sir,' he said. He turned away to the horses. 'Let's hope the wolves do not find us,' he muttered.

Wilson climbed up in his seat beside the driver and wrapped a cloak around him. The wind was cold for though spring was beginning, the grip of winter had not yet gone completely.

After they had travelled for some miles Maletov seemed to brighten up.

'It is only about three miles to the village now,' he said.

Wilson nodded. He decided that he had been right to push on after all and that the tales about wolves were the imaginings of the local farmers.

Suddenly Maletov hauled on his reins, bringing the horses to sudden stop. He stood up on his seat and looked around.

'What is it?' asked Wilson. 'What's wrong?'

'Shh,' hissed the *yemstchik*. 'Be quiet.'

Wilson sat watching his companion. The silence

of the forest was almost ominous. The wind whispered in the trees, but otherwise Wilson could hear nothing at all.

'I knew it,' said Maletov grimly.

'What?' asked Wilson.

'Wolves,' said the *yemstchik*. 'And they have scented game.'

Wilson still could not hear anything. Then a distant yelp came to his ears, seeming to come from behind them. Then he heard a second yelp.

The *yemstchik* sat down in his seat and picked up his whip. He cracked it over the heads of the horses, which set off at a fast walk. A second crack of the whip hurried the horses into a trot.

'Let's hope the wolves are not after us,' said Maletov, keeping his eyes on the road ahead, 'but there is a shotgun and ammunition under the seat in case they are.'

Wilson reached beneath the seat and pulled out a large shotgun. Finding a pouch of ammunition, Wilson loaded the shot into the gun and sat with it on his knees. The trotting horses set a brisk pace through the forest, but Maletov glanced over his shoulder and cracked his whip to urge the horses to a faster pace.

Before long, Wilson could hear the sound of wolves over the noise of the coach.

'They are gaining on us,' he said nervously.

Maletov nodded and glanced back along the twisting forest road. 'They are on our scent all right. Keep an eye out behind us.'

Wilson swivelled in his seat and kept his eyes fixed

on the dark forest behind the coach. The sun was beginning to set and the shadows of the woodlands became darker and deeper. The yelping and howling of the wolves came louder and clearer. Wilson knew that they could not be far behind now.

Suddenly the dark shape of a wolf bounded round a corner in the track, followed by a second, then a third and fourth. Soon a whole mass of wolves came into sight. Wilson nudged the driver.

'Here they come,' he said.

The *yemstchik* glanced backwards then turned to his horses and whipped them into a canter. 'Try to hit the leaders,' he said, 'that might slow them down a bit.'

Wilson took careful aim and fired. The gun roared, but had no effect. He had missed.

Reloading the gun Wilson raised it to his shoulder. The wolves were closer now. He fired and the leader went crashing to the ground. In seconds the following wolves were pouncing on it, tearing it apart in their hunger.

Wilson stared in surprise, not expecting the wolves to eat each other. Maletov had been right, the wolves were certainly very hungry. Within seconds the dead wolf had been torn apart and eaten. Again the pack came on, howling and yelping as they charged.

When the wolves drew close again, Wilson fired. He brought down a wolf, but this time the pack did not halt. Maletov glanced back, then cracked his whip savagely and shouted loudly, sending the horses bounding forwards at the gallop. With a

sudden whinny, the horses caught the scent of the wolves and bolted forwards at breakneck speed.

The sudden surge almost threw Wilson from his perch. Desperately he grabbed hold of the arm rest. If he fell amongst the wolves he would be dead in seconds. Luckily he checked his fall, and scrambled back to his seat.

The chill wind blew through his hair as the horses plunged on through the forest. Reloading the gun, Wilson blazed away at the pack, now snapping around the wheels of the carriage. A wolf somer-saulted to the ground as the shot struck him, disappearing into the darkness as the coach raced on.

'Fire carefully,' shouted the *yemstchik* as he cracked his whip again, 'keep the vermin away from the horses. If a horse goes down we are dead men.'

Wilson loaded his gun again. Turning in his seat, he saw the lead wolves drawing level with the galloping horses. One of the wolves lunged, snapping at the heels of a horse. Whipping the gun to his shoulder, Wilson aimed and fired. The gun crashed out, the flash of the muzzle bathing the scene in a vivid red light. The wolf took the shot in the back and fell to the ground.

A second wolf took its place. Before Wilson could reload, the wolf had reached the horse, sinking its teeth into the thrashing leg. Hurriedly raising his gun, Wilson fired again, the wolf twisted sideways, crashing to the ground in front of the coach wheels.

The horses galloped harder than ever, dashing through the dark forest at a speed which frightened Wilson almost as much as the wolves. If the coach struck a hole or stone in the road, it would overturn, throwing them to the ground at the mercy of the wolves. Yet Maletov did not slacken the pace for a moment. Whipping the horses harder with every moment he seemed determined to drive the plunging horses to the limits of their strength.

Raising his gun yet again, Wilson saw the wolves were dropping back. They were no longer with the horses, but snapping around the wheels of the coach. Seconds later the wolves had dropped back further and given up the chase. Wilson nudged Maletov who glanced back and smiled with relief.

'Outrun them at last,' he gasped. 'I thought for a moment that we were not going to make it.'

For some distance further the *yemstchik* kept the horses at full gallop, then allowed them to ease back into a canter and then a trot. Coming round a bend in the road, lights came into view through the darkness. They had reached the village and were safe.

Later that night, talking around the fire with the locals, Wilson and the *yemstchik* recounted the story of their fight with the wolves. One of the old men nodded his head at the story.

'I remember many years ago,' he said, 'I went hunting with Duke Aleski in Siberia one winter. There were forty of us in all, with the lords, cooks and servants. One day we ran into a pack of wolves over a hundred strong. We leapt into the horse-drawn sledges and galloped off, but the wolves gave chase. The beasts managed to drag down three of the sledges. They ate everything, the horses, the people, even the leather harness from the horses.

Less than half of us came back from that hunting trip. The wolves can be very dangerous when they are hungry.'

o o o

Throughout most of the world wolves are now very much rarer than they were when William Wilson travelled through Russia. It is unlikely that giant packs, over a hundred in number, are formed these days, even when hunger causes different packs to hunt together. However, smaller packs still roam many areas of the world, particularly in the more remote areas of Canada, Europe and Asia.

These wolves normally find enough food in the wild, but attacks on humans continue to be reported. One evening in April 1962 the farmers of the Turkish village of Buca finished work for the day, as usual, and returned home from the fields. They had no reason to expect that this night would be any different from any other, but it was to turn into a night of terror and death.

As dusk fell on Buca, the villagers sat in their houses talking to each other or reading. As dusk turned to night a long, low howl swept through the valley.

'What was that?' asked Mustapha.

His younger brother, Ibrahim, looked up from playing with some toys. 'What was what?' he asked.

The howl sounded out again.

'It's a wolf,' said Mehmet, Mustapha's father. 'I

had better check that the cattle shed is properly locked.' He put his coat on, picked up a lantern and slipped out of the door. Moments later he came back.

'The old wooden bolt is broken,' he said, 'can you boys come and give me a hand?'

'Father,' said Mustapha in a worried voice. 'There's something by the barn.'

Mehmet looked up to see what appeared to be a pair of bright lights hovering by the barn door. He looked more closely and realized that the lights were the eyes of a wolf reflecting the light of the lantern. A second pair of eyes joined the first, and then a third.

'Stay close to me,' Mehmet told his sons, 'and we should be all right.' Mehmet picked the axe from his tool box. He was beginning to be worried. Wolves did not usually come this close to the village and to man.

'Come on boys,' said Mehmet, 'let's get back to the house.'

Slowly Mehmet edged towards the house, keeping a careful eye on the wolves which were watching him from only a few metres away. He had nearly reached the door when Mustapha shouted 'Look out!'

There was a sudden blur of movement beside Mehmet and a cry of pain from Ibrahim. Mehmet whirled around to see a wolf dragging Ibrahim away into the darkness. He screamed loudly and a neighbour, Isad, ran out of his house. He saw the wolves gathered around and stopped short.

Isad stared at Mehmet in horror.

'What is going on?' he asked. 'What are the wolves up to?'

'I don't know,' said Mehmet. 'Let's get the other men together.'

Mehmet bustled Mustapha into the house and told his wife to bolt the door. Then he and Isad ran around the village telling everyone what had happened and asking them to come to help. Soon three dozen men were gathered in the village street armed with axes, knives and scythes.

Mehmet led the men out into the dark fields after the wolves. They found the tracks of the animals, but there was no sign of Ibrahim. Mehmet heard the wolves in the forest and, fearing that his son was dead, he led the men towards the trees.

Suddenly a long, loud howl came from the forest. A second wolf yelped, then a third and soon the men thought that every wolf in the forest was giving voice. The men stopped in fear and bunched together, gripping their weapons tightly.

Then the pack was upon them. Snarling and howling the wolves dashed forwards. One man was thrown over as a wolf slammed into his chest. Only a swift thrust by a man with a pitchfork drove the animal away. Another man was bitten badly in the leg, before he could kill the beast attacking him. Mehmet slashed at a wolf with his axe, breaking its back with the blow.

After several seconds of savage fighting, the wolves scampered back to the forest. The men were badly shaken, some of them were bleeding from cuts and bites. One man lay moaning on the ground as his friends stared with frightened eyes into the darkness, looking for the wolves.

'Get back to the village,' said Mehmet. 'It's too dangerous out here.' Quickly the men hurried to the village, carrying the wounded between them. They could hear the wolves howling in the forest nearby. The men were frightened to stay in their homes alone so they collected all their families and locked themselves in the biggest house.

The wolves continued to call and an hour later came back to the village. They prowled through the streets, nosing around the empty houses until they found the house with the people in. Scratching at the doors and windows, the wolves circled the house, howling loudly.

Inside the villagers huddled together, and stared anxiously at the doors. Some of the men stood beside the doors armed with axes and scythes in case the wolves managed to break in. But the doors held firm and the wolves stayed outside. After an hour or so the wolves left the house and drifted back to the forest. The villagers heard the calls of the pack as it moved further and further away between the trees.

Aidan Chambers
Haunted Houses £1.99

*Out of the darkness they creep, filling empty hallways
with echoes of deathly footsteps, mournful howling
and shrieks of terror . . .*

Enter these haunted houses and discover their hor-
rifying hidden secrets. Here are ten chilling true
stories to take you deep inside the places where
people have seen ghosts, heard them and, most
frightening of all, *felt* them.

This Place is Haunted £2.50

Haunted houses, gruesome groans, the moans of
tortured spirits that lurk in forgotten cellars; eerie
shuffling and mysterious sounds in the night . . .

Get ready to meet your nightmares in these terrifying true stories of haunted places, and you'll soon
be longing for morning light.

All Pan books are available at your local bookshop or newsagent, or can be ordered direct from the publisher. Indicate the number of copies required and fill in the form below.

Send to: **CS Department, Pan Books Ltd., P.O. Box 40,
            Basingstoke, Hants.   RG21 2YT.**

or phone: 0256 469551 (Ansaphone), quoting title, author
             and Credit Card number.

Please enclose a remittance* to the value of the cover price plus: 60p for the first book plus 30p per copy for each additional book ordered to a maximum charge of £2.40 to cover postage and packing.

*Payment may be made in sterling by UK personal cheque, postal order, sterling draft or international money order, made payable to Pan Books Ltd.

Alternatively by Barclaycard/Access:

Card No.

Signature:

Applicable only in the UK and Republic of Ireland.

While every effort is made to keep prices low, it is sometimes necessary to increase prices at short notice. Pan Books reserve the right to show on covers and charge new retail prices which may differ from those advertised in the text or elsewhere.

NAME AND ADDRESS IN BLOCK LETTERS PLEASE:

....

Name ————————————————————————

Address ————————————————————————

————————————————————————————

————————————————————————————

————————————————————————————
                                                          3/87